THE 250 SALES QUESTIONS TO
CLOSE THE DEAL

Stephan Schiffman

Adams Media
Avon, Massachusetts

Published by
Adams Media, an F+W Publications Company
57 Littlefield Street, Avon, MA 02322. U.S.A.
www.adamsmedia.com

ISBN 10: 1-59337-280-9
ISBN 13: 978-1-59337-280-4
Printed in Canada.

J I H G F E D C B

Library of Congress Cataloging-in-Publication Data
Schiffman, Stephan.
The 250 sales questions to close the deal / Stephan Schiffman.
p. cm.
ISBN 1-59337-280-9
1. Selling—Handbooks, manuals, etc. I. Title: Two hundred and fifty sales
questions to close the deal. II. Title.

HF5438.25.S3335 2005
658.85—dc22
2004026359

This publication is designed to provide accurate and authoritative information
with regard to the subject matter covered. It is sold with the understanding that
the publisher is not engaged in rendering legal, accounting, or other professional advice. If legal advice or other expert assistance is required, the services
of a competent professional person should be sought.
　　—From a *Declaration of Principles* jointly adopted by a Committee of the
American Bar Association and a Committee of Publishers and Associations

Many of the designations used by manufacturers and sellers to distinguish their
products are claimed as trademarks. Where those designations appear in this
book and Adams Media was aware of a trademark claim, the designations have
been printed with initial capital letters.

This book is available at quantity discounts for bulk purchases.
For information, please call 1-800-289-0963.

Contents

Acknowledgments

My thanks go out to all the people whose help made this book possible: Brandon Toropov, Steve Bookbinder, Lynne Einleger, Amy Stagg, Scott Forman, Tina Bradshaw, Alan Koval, Surendra Sewsankar, George Richardson, Stacia Skinner, Art Jackson, David Rivera, and everyone else at D.E.I. Management Group. As always, thank you Daniele, Jennifer, and Anne.

Introduction

Superior questioning skills are a prerequisite of any successful selling career. In this book, I've tried to share what I've learned about questioning in the sales interview over the past quarter of a century. I've focused in on 250 essential sales questions . . . questions that, when asked intelligently and in the right setting, will help you build rapport, streamline your sales process, and, yes, *close more deals.*

As always, I'm interested in your comments on what follows. I hope you'll write to me with your insights and experiences.

Make it a productive day!

Stephan Schiffman

President

D.E.I. Management Group

888 7th Avenue, 9th Floor

New York, NY 10106

contactus@dei-sales.com

Chapter One

Six Kinds of Questions

This book is designed to help you ask questions that move you closer to closing the deal. It offers 250 questions designed to help you travel relentlessly toward that goal. The questions are arranged into six distinct categories.

1. Questions that help you initiate contact and build a rapport with the prospect—*Chapter Two*.
2. Questions that help you figure out what the other person does (you can't sell effectively if you don't know this)—*Chapters Three, Four, and Five*.
3. Questions that help you secure a Next Step with the prospect—*Chapters Six and Seven*.
4. Questions that help you identify the right presentation—*Chapter Eight*.

5. Questions that help you deal with setbacks or obstacles in the sale—*Chapter Nine*.

6. Questions that will help you formalize the decision to use what your product or service offers—and negotiate the best deal—*Chapter Ten*.

Going Beyond "Magic Questions"

When I train salespeople, I often ask what kinds of questions they think are the most important in the sales process. A good many of them tell me that they want to focus on "killer questions"—questions that supposedly "force the issue" or "close the sale." These sorts of questions typically sound like this:

- "What do I have to do to get you into a Dodge Viper?"
- "When should we start?"
- "Do you want it in blue, or in yellow?"

Basically, these are questions that sound like—and have even been described as—"closing questions." It's like people think there are magic words they can say that will turn a skeptical prospect into a customer.

The sad, and often overlooked, truth is that these questions alienate prospects. They will close only those sales where the person has already more or less decided to buy. These are *not* the kinds of questions you and I will be exploring in this book.

Selling is a process, and a fairly complex one. No one single question recited from memory during a few short seconds is likely to secure the deal for you. That's the bad news. Here's the good news: *Intelligent questions posed as part of a larger process* can and will win you the business. And that's what we'll be exploring together in this book.

Selling as a Process

Think of selling as a process, a relationship that emerges over time.

Like all useful processes, good selling has a goal. What is the final stage of the sale? Typically, the salespeople I talk to will tell me that the final stage is the close, and that is certainly accurate enough. But it is also true that it is only salespeople who are focused on "closing" a deal. From the buyer's perspective, the initial decision to agree to work with us is actually a decision to "use" what we have to offer.

So, instead of focusing obsessively on the word "close," I prefer to think of the final stage of the sale as the prospect's decision to use what we have to offer. The prospect decides to use our product or service—that's the direction where we want our questions to take us.

Let's start from that point and work backward. I want my new customer to use me as a resource—not just today, but hopefully forever. That is the ideal result of the sales situation. Here's a brief description of what I call the *"Makes Sense" Selling Model*. It shows the sales process as it *should* work:

1. Open (takes little time)
2. Gather info (the most time!)
3. Plan (little time)
4. Close (hardly any time!): The point where we say, "Makes sense to me—what do you think?" (That's the ultimate question to close the deal, by the way.)

And here are a few things to remember about this model:

- People only buy what makes sense to them
- Your plan must be based on what they do
- 75 percent of the work comes before your presentation

What "Makes Sense"

What questions can we ask to "make" the person decide to use us? There really are none. In fact, the only reason people ever buy anything is because it makes sense for them to do so—makes sense from their point of view.

Stop for a moment and think about the last time you purchased anything from a high-pressure salesperson. Even if you happened to run into someone who used all kinds of fancy closing "tricks" in an attempt to get you to buy, and even if after hearing one of those closing tricks you did decide to buy from him or her, my guess is that the reason you did so is that it made sense for you to buy from that person.

Perhaps your whole business is built around documents and copying—and perhaps your copier had once died during a rush period. You then had a busy period coming up, and a copier salesman happened to call or walk in the door. You took a glance at your deadlines, you took another glance at the copier salesman, and you listened to what he had to say. Half an hour later, you agreed that it made sense to get a new copier. So you bought from him.

No matter what the salesman said, you bought because it made sense for you to do so. Whether it will make sense for you to buy from the same copier salesman *again* is another question.

The ultimate, and most effective, closing technique, the single question that is likeliest to win you the deal, sounds like this:

Well, Ms. Prospect, that is what we are proposing. It makes sense to me . . . what do you think?

This is the only "closing technique" that I teach. It is the question that every other question in this book is pointing you toward.

This closing strategy is tremendously effective—far more

effective than the silly, manipulative questions people usually ask, because it isolates for us exactly what is going on in the relationship.

If the person we are talking to is someone who is already in the marketplace—such as the person whose copier has just gone down—the "makes sense" question really will do at least as good a job of delivering the business to you as the "closing trick" questions, and probably a far better one. This is because it helps you to isolate and strategize any obstacles that still exist. If the reason you're suggesting doesn't make sense, the person will usually tell you exactly why. Then you can explore those avenues with more "do-based" questions.

Three Groups to Sell To

Can you see where I'm going with this? Let's look more closely at the people we're trying to sell to. We can separate them into three distinct categories.

IMPs are people who are already IN THE MARKET-PLACE. These are people who are actively looking for our product or service. If we were to ask these people, "What do you need?" they would give us an exact answer, because they have already determined that they do in fact "need" something they have not yet obtained. They're actively searching. As you can see, this is a small group.

EMPs are people who are ENTERING THE MAR-KETPLACE. These people have made a similar decision, but they do not have the same sense of urgency that there is with those in the IMP group. They typically say, "We're looking," or "We're comparing." This is not a very large group, either.

The third and biggest group is the **CCs** (CLOISTERED CUSTOMERS). They are people who are presently outside our marketplace, working with someone else. We generally have to contact CCs ourselves. This larger group is where we want to go for growth—by helping them do what they are trying to do better. But it's more difficult to start these relationships! These people will only respond if we find out what their unique goals are and show how working with us will help to turn those goals into reality.

The IMP and EMP groups are too small for us to be able to count on for continued sales. We must constantly reach out to people in the CC group to build our base of prospects and customers.

Beyond Order Taking

The IMP kind of discussion—the conversation with the person whose copier just broke down, and who wants another one right now—doesn't happen enough for us to count on it to support our lifestyle. In fact, this is a "sale" only in the technical sense. It is actually a good deal closer to order taking. There is very little work or analysis involved in the purchase decision. And a quick decision to work with us may not mean that the person has decided to work with us forever, which is our goal.

All the same, it does produce revenue, and it happens because it makes sense to the other person.

BUT . . . suppose the person is *not* yet in the marketplace? Suppose the person is *entering* the marketplace, or is a customer committed to some other vendor? Is there any way we can sell to such a person? Sure, but we have to find the right plan. We have to determine what the right presentation, or reason for buying, looks like. We have to find the plan that really does make more sense to the other person than continuing to do what he or she is already doing.

We have to challenge the status quo, and we can't do that if we don't know which plan will make sense.Conversely, if we have done our homework and have isolated exactly what really does make sense to that person, we will have identified the one plan that matches up with what is going on in his or her world. If we find that plan, we may be able to make the case for changing the current situation, and the reason to change will make sense to the other person.

This is not necessarily easy—but it can be done. (At my company we have a saying: "Your #1 competitor is the status quo.") Typically, this process happens only when the person commits to an extended series of conversations, which means that we have to make a point of strategizing clear Next Steps with the person we're talking to (more on those later). If the person isn't committed to investing time and energy in developing the plan with us, we're not really moving forward in the sales process! Why is it so important to win a Next Step from the prospect and engage this person in a dialogue about the plan we're developing? Because there are a million potential plans that we *could* talk about. Our job is to identify the ONE that makes sense. And that's where effective questioning comes in.

My experience is that the vast majority of salespeople make presentations based on what makes sense to them as salespeople, and not what makes sense to the other person. As a matter of fact, most of the salespeople I run into have very little idea what is actually going on in their prospects' lives. How do I know that they know very little about the situations their prospects face? *Because they make the same presentation over and over and over again.*

Same Presentation Syndrome
If you have ever had a salesperson ask you a few perfunctory questions and then move right into a "presentation" that has

obviously been delivered 100 or 1,000 times before, you know exactly what I'm talking about. My guess is that you have also had a salesperson sit you down, spread a brochure in front of you, and "walk you through" the items on the brochure, element by element, as though you were not capable of reading them for yourself. These are signs of a salesperson who has not gathered unique information about the prospect, and they are very common signs indeed.

In order to make sure that what we present really will make sense to this person—enough sense to change what they're doing right now—we have to ask questions about what the other person does. I very intentionally say "what the person does," as opposed to "what the person needs." In the world of sales, I have found, there many misperceptions about words like "needs" and "problems" and "pain."

In this book, you will be dealing with questions that will help you identify what is currently happening in the prospect's world, and you will not find me recommending any questions that encourage you to "probe" for needs, pain, or problems. We have to focus on what the person and the organization are *doing* and to leave aside our own predispositions about what the pain is, what the problem is, what the need is.

The reason for this is simple. If I ask what a person needs, that person is very likely to tell me he or she has no need whatsoever. After all, if the prospect had a need, he or she would have called me rather than me calling him or her!

The information I get when I ask what the person "needs" is likely to be incomplete, or even inaccurate.

Similarly, if I ask about pain, I may get some information, but I still will not get the whole picture. In other words, if there is a particular dissatisfaction or skill gap or deficit in whatever they are currently using right now, *and* if the "pain" happens to be on the person's mind, *and* if the person happens to be willing to share it with me, then I may get some information I can build a proposal around. But this is a very small portion of the "pie" that represents the environment the person is facing.

What if I ask the person to describe pressing business problems that he or she faces or will face in the future? What if I build my proposal around those problem issues? I might get a decent idea of what is going on in that person's world, but I will not get the whole picture. Even if you discover everything about the person's pains, needs, and problems, you will have only learned about certain parts of their situation—the parts that are currently causing pain and problems. You won't be getting the whole picture.What about the rest of your contact's situation—the things that don't fit in the categories of pains, needs, or problems? What's going on there? If I only ask about "needs," I don't know—and if you've only been asking the types of questions mentioned above, neither do you.

What if, on the other hand, I build my questions around what the person is doing right now, what he plans to do in the future, who he is doing it with, why he is doing it that way, when he does it, and so on? By doing that, I will get a much more accurate and complete picture of what that person is facing.

As a matter of fact, I will uncover everything that I would have uncovered by means of asking about needs, pain, or problems. There is nothing of importance that cannot be covered by what the person actually does. Using this method, I will also get some more significant insight into what the person is trying to accomplish, which is really what matters. The other advantage of the do-based selling philosophy is that it helps me to phrase the right questions during any negotiation discussions.

Verification

Even after asking questions like these, however, I have to be sure that my presentation really is aligned with what is likely to make sense to the person. That is why I have to incorporate a verification substep to make absolutely sure that what I am going to recommend really does make sense. The verification substep fits into our selling model after we have gathered information, and before we create a plan that we can present. This is my chance to confirm my assumptions before I make a formal recommendation. It is an extremely important step, one that most salespeople skip.

Why Presentations Fail

The experience at our company is that 90 percent of the sales presentations that do not turn into revenue have some kind of problem in the information-gathering phase.

My own personal philosophy is I would rather make fewer presentations that have a higher likelihood of actually closing. Wouldn't you?

Before we gather the information, of course, we have to ask questions during the opening phase of the relationship. We have to initiate the discussion, set the first appointment, and establish a little bit of rapport with the person before we jump into our question phase. Without this kind of discussion, we really can't move forward to the other questions. You can't walk in and say, "What kind of copier are you looking for?" before you shake the person's hand, introduce yourself, and make a little small talk. In the sales model, we have illustrated, these types of rapport-building questions should be used during the short opening period. So what kinds of questions have we identified? Look at them again:

1. Questions that help you initiate contact and build rapport with a prospect.
2. Questions about what the other person does. (By the way, this is where we want to spend most of our time with the

prospect. Not surprisingly, the majority of questions in this book are designed to help you identify what the person does.)

3. Questions that help you secure a Next Step with the prospect.
4. Questions that help you identify the right presentation by verifying your information.
5. Questions that help you deal with setbacks or obstacles in the sale.
6. Questions that will help you formalize the decision to use what your product or service offers—and negotiate the best deal.

These are the questions that will move us forward in the sales process . . . and also move us forward in the relationship once the prospect becomes a customer.

Remember—there is no single question that will transform an unwilling contact into a buyer. But there are questions and strategies you can use to uncover what is really happening in a person's world and make them more likely to share the information that will allow you to make a high percentage "shot"—and improve your closing ratios.

The Sales Continuum

There are four levels on the sales continuum, and the kinds of questions we ask determine where we are headed on that continuum. The higher we move with the customer on the sales continuum, the more "do-based" questions we ask, the better our information gets, and the more valuable the relationship becomes.

■ The first (and lowest) level is the SELLER. This level features virtually no trust or information; it's typically a "one-time-sale" mentality on both sides of the transaction.

- The SUPPLIER relationship features a little trust and a little information. You're "in the Rolodex," and future business is a possibility, but not a sure thing.
- The VENDOR relationship is higher still. It features significant levels of trust and information, there is predictable repeat business, and you help the customer develop criteria for doing business and resolving challenges.
- At the highest level is the PARTNER/RESOURCE relationship. Here, there are extremely high levels of trust and information; you function as a strategic partner, and you and the customer are mutually dependent on each other for success. At the PARTNER/RESOURCE level, you have easy access to all key players within the organization.

Most of us go back and forth between Vendor and Supplier. Our goal should be to take the time to figure out what's really happening in the other person's world, where we really are with our prospects and clients, and how we can move forward. Our goal should be to use "do-based" questions to strive toward the Partner/Resource relationship.

Chapter Two

Questions That Initiate Contact and Build Rapport with a Prospect

We saw in Chapter One that the first category of questions is made up of those that seek to establish initial contact and build some kind of rapport with the other person.

The most common means of establishing initial contact is through the cold prospecting call, although this is by no means the only way to reach out to someone.

Prospecting calls to businesspeople today are generally *not* standardized. What salespeople say varies dramatically from call to call, even when the same sales-person is dialing the phone. Perhaps just as important, these salespeople do not identify basic questions—that is, proven questions that the salesperson can and should use to develop a single standard calling approach, or script.

I am not going to try to give you a complete breakdown of the prospecting call in this book. That is something that is cov-ered in some depth in my book, *Cold Calling Techniques (That Really Work!)*, published by Adams Media. However, I do want to share with you a story about a woman we trained in Canada several years ago who realized that effective cold calling basi-cally can be boiled down to a single question. That question looks like this:

Question 1: What I'd like to do is get together with you this coming Tuesday at 10:00—does that make sense?

Obviously, you cannot spring that question on somebody within the first five seconds of a call, so there is a little bit of preparation that must precede it.

For the record, here is an abbreviated version of a calling approach that leads up to that question:

> Hello, Mr. Prospect, this is Steve Schiffman calling from D.E.I. Management Group. I'm not sure if you've heard of us, but we're one of the largest sales training companies in the United States and we work with firms such as This Company, That Company, and The Other Company. The reason I'm call-ing you today specifically is that we just completed a program with Big Company that helped them to dramatically increase their first appointment totals, and I'd really like to meet with you to show you the success that we had with them. I'd like to get together with you next Tuesday at 10:00. Does that make sense?

Notice that this is a standardized approach, which means that it is a script that I memorize and can deliver over and over in exactly the same way. It always leads directly to that closing question.

Great Results!

Now the woman whom we trained in Canada had the following experience with the script that I just shared with you: She liked it, she wrote one that mirrored it, and she even practiced it. But during the time that I was training her, she did not have the script down cold. Not only that, she did not remember all the techniques I had taught her for turning around initial negative responses. (You will not be surprised, I think, to learn that a negative response is something we should be prepared for during the conference call.)

The point I am getting at is that the only thing that she really remembered was the question, *Can we get together this coming Tuesday at 2:00—does that make sense?* And she got great results!

By the way—for me, a "prospect" is someone who agrees, in person, to move through the sales process with me. So that means that someone really isn't a prospect until I actually meet with her face-to-face and she agrees to meet with me again. (As you can tell, I do the majority of my selling in person.)

So what you have just seen is a single question that really can transform your entire sales career if you practice it. Try it. Build a script along the lines of the short sample script that you have read here; practice it relentlessly until you could recite it if you were awakened from a sound sleep; and make sure you always return the call to that question:

I'd like to get together with you next Tuesday at 2:00— does that make sense?

I should warn you, however, of one very important point: This technique only works if you are asking for an appointment Tuesday at 2:00. (Just kidding.)

Question 2: Have you ever done any (sales training) before?

The question you just read is the one that I am always ready to use in my industry when I am reaching out to a new lead for the very first time by telephone. During these calls, as you might expect, it is quite common for me to encounter resistance or interruption. In fact, it happens so often that I am interrupted, or that I hear a negative response, that I know I have to prepare for that possibility. One of the things I do is to turn around that objection so that I can refocus the conversation. Very often, I will refocus the conversation by asking the question you just read. Understand, I am not attempting to make the prospecting call a long, drawn-out interview of the person I have reached out to by phone—the relationship simply is not old enough yet for me to gather information on the phone, and most of my sales process happens face-to-face. I just want to regain control of the call, and I want to find out something very basic about the company I'm calling.

As I said, during the initial conversation, I fully expect to be interrupted. When this happens, I could say, "I would love to show you what I have done for the Big Company; why don't we get together on Tuesday at 2:00?" And our training has proven that, statistically, you will get a higher number of appointments by following this very basic approach than you will by simply yammering on about how wonderful your products are. A focused conversation—that is to say, a conversation based on gathering a commitment for a Next Step—will always get you better results than an unfocused conversation.

But there is a more subtle, and, I believe, more effective way to refocus a conversation, and that is by means of something that I call "the Ledge." And when I say "Ledge," what I really mean is a strategy for establishing a foothold in the initial conversation with the sales contact.

The Ledge in Action

So, let's say I'm the salesperson. I call you and I say:

"I would love to show you what I have done for the Big Company, why don't we get together on Tuesday at 2:00?"

And then you say to me:

"Steve, I am really not interested at all."

I can then use the Ledge to get a foothold in the conversation by turning around the objection and immediately asking a question of my own. Here is what it looks like.

"You know, a lot of other people have said that they were not interested in what my company did, until they saw how we could increase their total base of first appointments and increase total revenue. Just out of curiosity, have you ever done any sales training before?"

Now it might sound as though, by posing that question, I am interested in gathering as much information as I possibly can about this person, and then perhaps even trying to close the sale over the phone. But, in fact, my only aim is to redirect the conversation and to get some kind of positive response from the other person.

If the person says, "No, we have never really done any sales training before," I can then turn around and say, "Well, you know, we have worked with a lot of companies that have not yet done sales training, but when they saw what we had to offer, they decided that it really did make sense for their team. Why don't we get together next Tuesday at 2:00?"

On the other hand, if the person says, "Yes, we have

done sales training before," and then tells me what sort of sales training they have done, I can then say, "You know, it is interesting you mentioned that, because we have worked with a lot of companies that have done that sort of training before, and they found that what we have to offer in terms of first-appointment training really does complement what they do. I would love to get together and show you what we did for ABC Company. Can we meet next Tuesday at 2:00?"

YOUR QUESTIONING STRATEGY

By focusing your prospecting call and by using the Ledge to refocus the conversation, or to get away from a situation where the prospector is trying to interview over the phone, you can place the emphasis where it needs to be for field salespeople: setting up a face-to-face meeting. If somebody is not willing to meet with you face-to-face, and you sell in person, you can rest assured that you are not *dealing with a prospect*.

By the way, telesales professionals can use the Ledge to refocus the call—instead of asking for an appointment, they simply ask the next question they're trying to get answered.

Note that the prospecting conversation always returns to this initial question: Can I meet with you at a certain specific date and time?

Question 3: Why February?

This is a very powerful question. Even though it seems quite basic, it is one of the best ways to avoid prolonged bouts of telephone tag with prospective leads.

Here's how the conversation goes. You call someone up and say who you are and explain why you want to get together, and then you ask directly for the appointment, as I have suggested. At that point, the person's obstacle comes, not in the form of an outright objection, but rather in the form of a stall. Let us say that it is November, and the person tells you, "Gee, that sounds very interesting. Why don't you give me a call in February, and we'll get together then."

To be sure, you certainly should be ready to specify and mark down a certain date, say February 15, and then call back appropriately at that point. However, before you do that, you should find out exactly what is behind the date that the person has proposed. You are well within your rights to say, "I'd be happy to do that . . . but just out of curiosity, why the middle of February? What's happening between now and then?"

The answer you receive will tell you a great deal about the true nature of the objection you've been presented with. If the person says, "We are going through an incredibly busy period, and our customer base peaks in December and January," you should write that down in your notes, and use it as a point of entry to the next conversation. Now you know something about the business! If, on the other hand, the person tells you, "I'm just incredibly busy now and I think things will have calmed down by then," the odds are good that you are simply looking at a stall, and that the person is looking for a polite way to put you off.

Question 4: When we spoke back in November, you suggested that I give you a call today so we could get together and so I can show you what we have done for XYZ Company. Is Monday at 10:00 a good time?

This is the question I ask when I am making a follow-up call along the lines discussed above. Notice that I do not make the assumption that the person needs to be reacquainted with my call. The reason I am calling is to follow through on what we discussed last time, namely the person's willingness to meet me in February.

Remember, sales is all about moving relationships forward. That is what we are trying to do. So when somebody says to me, "I'll speak to you in mid-February," or suggests that I call him to set up a meeting, that is precisely what I am going to do. I will not beat around the bush, reintroduce myself, or apologize for taking any time out of the person's day. To the contrary, I am going to assume that the discussion we had last time is still valid, and as for that apology for the meeting, specify a particular time and place. If the person has questions about what the call is about, I will be happy to answer them. But, as a means of opening the call, I am going to ask forthrightly for the appointment we discussed the last time around.

Question 5: Can I get your advice?

There are any number of reasons for scheduling a face-to-face meeting with a prospect. Among the most creative is a request for information about whether what you sell is applicable within that person's industry.

Let's say you are trying to sell for the first time to a group you have never sold before—accountants, for example. And suppose that you have successfully sold to another group that the group you are trying to reach would have heard of—banks, let's say. Here is what your initial call could sound like:

> Hi, Mr. Jones, this is Steve Schiffman calling from D.E.I. Management Group. I'm not sure whether or not you've heard of us, but we're a sales training company here in New York

City and we work with companies like The Blah Blah Banking Group. The reason I'm calling you today specifically is that I'm trying to figure out whether or not a program we did for Fleet Bank has any application whatsoever within the accounting industry. I'd like to get together with you to show you what we did for Fleet Bank and get your feedback on it, to see if we should be marketing to people in your industry. Can we get together this coming Tuesday at 10:00?

Notice that this is a very low-pressure way to sell. It is an intriguing variation on the standard call, one that you may find helpful when you are branching out into new markets in which you can appeal to your contact as "one professional to another."

Question 6: Why don't we just get together?

This is an extremely effective question you can use to overcome objections, stalls, and long-winded responses from people whom you are prospecting on the phone. The advantage of the question lies in its straightforward nature. I cannot tell you the number of times that I have used this question to "cut to the chase" and deliver a friendly reminder to a new contact that the point of my call is to schedule a face-to-face meeting.

This question basically says, "Shouldn't we advance this relationship to the Next Step?" If the answer is a definitive no, you are going to find out then and there. If the answer is maybe, you are going to find out the reasons there is some hesitation to getting together or to moving forward toward the Next Step. If the answer is yes, you are going to find out instantly; at that point you will pull out your appointment book, set the time and date, and politely get off the phone.

Question 7: So I've got us down for (date) and (time), right?

Ask this question and then get off the phone. Politely, of course!

It is important to *conclude* the phone conversation with the prospect once you have set the appointment, however you ask to do so. If you set the appointment and then keep talking, only one thing can happen—the person can decide it does not really make sense to meet with you!

Question 8: Can I give a free speech in front of your group?

I have included this question because it is very easy for a president, CEO, marketing director, quality assurance director, or head of the local chamber of commerce to agree to. That's important because, if you are like most salespeople, you will want to set some other means of establishing initial contact with your prospects besides making cold calls. (Understand, I am not advocating that you avoid cold calling, just that you find ways to augment that method of prospecting.)

By delivering a thirty-minute to one-hour overview of your product or service, or about some aspect of what your company does, you will be engaging in what is, perhaps, the most "painless" method of prospecting out there. In any given group of 100 people who come to hear your free talk, approximately 25 percent of that group will self-qualify, and become a prospect of yours. In other words, you can expect one out of four people to come up to you after the talk, strike up a conversation, and at the end of the conversation you can expect to exchange business cards and establish some kind of Next Step with that person to discuss the possibility of doing business with you. This is a great method of prospecting for those who are comfortable delivering impromptu lectures or formal speeches, and/or conducting question-and-answer periods with potential buyers.

Find a way, at least once a month, to get in front of groups of people who could buy your product or service.

Question 9: Can I take you out to lunch?

I have a standing rule in my company: People who do not have any live sales prospects should have a minimum of three lunch appointments with potential prospects every business week. To understand the significance of that rule, I need to explain a couple of terms. First of all, a "prospect," as we have seen, is not necessarily someone with whom I wish to do business. Rather, it is someone who has agreed to talk about the prospect of doing business with me, and who is willing to set aside a specific date and time in his or her schedule in order to have that discussion.

Managing Prospects

The other thing you should understand is that my company is run according to a Prospect Management System, under which prospects have specific categories. First would be those who have agreed to meet with us for the very first time, even though such a person is technically not a prospect since we have not had a face-to-face meeting yet and he or she could still cancel. Another category is for those whom I have met once and am returning to meet again—I call this group *25 percent prospects*. In another column, there are those with whom I am quite certain I have isolated all the relevant information to develop a proposal—these are *50 percent prospects*. And then there are those who have given me a verbal commitment—*90 percent prospects.* All three groups of prospects—25 percent, 50 percent, and 90 percent—must be accompanied by clear Next Steps from the person with whom we are talking. So, for 50 percent prospects, the person might have agreed to meet with me in the next two weeks. But if someone puts me off by asking that I give him a call sometime six months from now, then I do not count that person as a prospect.

So, let's look back again at the rule that I make our salespeople follow, and that I advocate that sales managers all across the country make their salespeople follow. If you do not have any live prospects on your board—that is to say, no legitimate 25 percent, 50 percent, or 90 percent contacts who are meeting with you within the next, say, two weeks—then you *must* schedule face-to-face meetings with potential prospects by offering to take them out to lunch. Clearly, these people do not quite count as "real" prospects because they have not decided to schedule a Next Step beyond the first contact with us—but they do qualify as first appointments, and this is a particular type of first appointment that should be relatively easy to get.

A Variation on the First Appointment Call

This is, in the final analysis, a variation on the first appointment call that goes beyond, "I would like to meet with you next Monday at 10:00" and moves instead to "I would like to meet with you and take you out to lunch. Are you free Thursday?" To be sure, it is a significant investment of time, energy, and attention to offer to take someone out to lunch. I always suggest that people make these offers intelligently. You should only extend this offer of a lunch meeting—at which you will pick up the tab—to those contacts with whom you feel quite confident you could conceivably do business.

How do you determine whether or not you will likely be

able to do business with someone, especially during the very brief confines of a prospecting call? See the next question.

YOUR QUESTIONING STRATEGY

The prospecting call itself should be a fairly brief affair—no more than one to two minutes—assuming that you are not trying to close a sale over the phone. This is because your call has an optimal length, a duration that, if exceeded, will result in a steadily reduced likelihood of closing the appointment, and setting the date for the first meeting. In my experience, that length is one to two minutes.

Question 10: The Knockout Question

In almost all the questions you will read about in this book, you will find a specific structure and a clear indication of precisely what words you should say. When it comes to this question, however, there is really no way for me to give you that. This is the question you should ask very early in the relationship—perhaps during the initial prospecting call, but definitely before you get too far into the first meeting. It is a question that allows you to determine exactly how close this person comes to matching the profile of your "perfect" customer.

Please understand that I am not advocating that you subject the person on the other end of the line to an extended interview that will allow you to conduct a regression analysis about how well they match up with your 100 top clients. I am talking about a *single* question that will help you to understand whether or not this person matches your criteria and is worth meeting face-to-face.

There always is an inherent danger in telling people to build this question into their prospecting call, because the temptation is so strong to embark on an in-depth conversation with the prospect. As we have seen, if that is not your selling model, you want to keep the call clearly focused on one topic and one topic only: whether or not the person will meet with you at a specific date and time. However, I have found that with just a little bit of practice, people can learn to keep their calls focused and also deliver this very simple kind of question. In my industry, the sales training industry, the appropriate knockout question is quite direct and sounds like this:

"How many salespeople do you have?"

By asking a question like this, I can instantly determine whether this opportunity is worth scheduling my day around. If the person I am talking to has two salespeople, that is a good distance away from the ideal answer I want to get, which is usually a minimum of ten salespeople. I wouldn't take that person out to lunch.

If, on the other hand, the person tells me he or she is in charge of 250 salespeople, I know that this is potentially going to be a major deal, and I am going to need to bring references about some of the larger accounts with whom we have worked. In either event, I will get valuable information that will make it very clear to me whether or not I want to move forward with this prospect.

Using the Knockout Question as Your Ledge Question

You may recall that, earlier on, I suggested that you use a question like "Have you ever worked with a sales training company before?" to regain the initiative in the conversation, and to refocus it on the issue of whether or not the person would be willing to meet with me at a specific date and time.

That question is certainly a valid one to use for the Ledge Strategy, but you may eventually decide to use your "knockout question" as your Ledge question, simply because doing so will give you a great deal more information about the contact, and it will help you determine when you are looking at a situation where you really do not want to meet with the person face-to-face.

In Question 9, I suggested that, if you are having trouble getting prospects and have no actual prospects on your board, you commit to securing at least three lunch meetings per week. Obviously, you do not want to take anyone who picks up the phone out to lunch! Before you schedule the lunch date, you should get the person's answer to your own knockout question so you can determine whether or not it is a viable opportunity.

Your Questioning Strategy

Examples of effective knockout questions that we have heard in other industries include:

1. How much do you typically ship each week?
2. How many people in your office telecommute?
3. How often do you schedule meetings with video conferencing?
4. How many people do you have who use company cell phones?

Don't Skip the Knockout Question!

You can easily see the importance of determining the answer to a knockout question. The challenge is to make sure that you use it simply to determine whether or not the meeting is worthwhile, and avoid the mistake of engaging in a long discussion with the person about your product or service. I cannot emphasize the point enough: Unless your job is to close sales over the phone, you should not attempt to sell on the telephone as commission points.

This has been a (severely) compressed overview of the neglected art of establishing initial contact. In just a few pages, I have given you some of the highlights of my strategies for making effective cold calls. Since the focus of this book is on asking effective questions throughout the sales process, this brief overview will have to do, but I do want to make sure that you have the chance to employ these strategies and techniques as your entry point to the sales process with a new contact. There is a lot more to be said about prospecting by phone, and specifically about monitoring your numbers and taking control of your ratios. You may want to take a look at my book *Cold Calling Techniques (That Really Work!).*

Questions to Ask Yourself

You have seen, in the previous pages, how to use questions to initiate contact with a sales lead, and a few basic ideas on how to turn around the objections you will face over the phone when trying to set an appointment. You have seen how to focus closely on the goal of the call: mainly, setting the appointment—and I hope by this point you have an initial understanding of why we are asking all these questions in the first place: to try and move the sales process forward and to keep suggesting steps that "make sense" to the other person.

The next thing that salespeople typically say to me is this: "Okay—I've set the meeting. How do I open up the discussion once I get face-to-face? What should I do to establish and build rapport with the other person? How do I make sure that I am laying the correct foundation for eventually closing the sale?"

These are all important issues, and we will be dealing

with them in due course. What I want to focus on now, however, is the more basic issue of what questions you must ask *yourself* before you even go on a first meeting.

The vast majority of the questions proposed in this book, of course, are designed for you to ask the prospect. However, if you skip over the essential step of asking yourself some key questions, you will significantly diminish your chances of closing the sale. That is why I am going to ask you to pay very close attention to what follows in this chapter and to use it as a foundation for what follows in the rest of the book. If you skip these basic questions, and if you fail to pose them and answer them on your own before you go to the meeting with your prospect, you will, I am afraid, miss out on many sales opportunities.

Question 11: What do we sell?

You must be able to describe concisely the products and services that your organization offers. You must also be ready at a moment's notice to explain specifically how those products and services benefit your company's customers. If you cannot explain what your company does in the 30 seconds or so you are likely to have while riding in an elevator with a total stranger from one floor to the next, your answer to the question is too long. Work it out on a separate sheet of paper. Write it down in words that are comfortable for you to say. Say it out loud. Revise it. Time it. Practice this answer until you can deliver it confidently and with no variation whatsoever.

Question 12: What makes us different from the competition?

The person you are talking to may well have only one way of distinguishing potential vendors. For instance, he or she may look at the price and disregard all other factors. On the other hand, the person may decide to do business with a vendor based on the number of years that the company has been in business. It is imperative that you become familiar with all the differences between yourself and the competition and be ready to discuss them. This time, instead of developing a single answer as you did with the previous question, develop at least seven different answers to the question "What makes you different from your competition?" These answers can be brief or they can be long, but they must be compelling, and rooted in actual customer experiences.

Question 13: What makes us better than the competition?

You should be prepared to explain, briefly and with great energy, the primary reason your best customer bought from you, rather than from somebody else. If you do not know the answer to this question, you *must* find out the answer from your colleagues, from your sales manager, or from other sources within the company. If no one you talk to seems to know the answer to the question "Why did our No. 1 customer buy from us?" then put a request through to the president or CEO of the company. You will be surprised, I think, how quickly the answer comes back, and at the level of detail you get from the head of the company. Take initiative, do the research, and find out the specifics. If you are uncomfortable doing any of this or talking about the answer that you uncover, then you are definitely in the wrong job! A good salesperson *must* be able to explain what makes his or her company better than the competing company.

Question 14: How would I complete the following sentence: "Even though we are not always the least expensive option, people buy from us because . . ."?

The way you complete this question, of course, may overlap somewhat with the answer that you gave to the question about why your company is better than the competition. That is fine. However, you must be willing to explain your value as both tangible and intangible benefits, along with the practical reasons people have chosen to focus on something other than price in order to develop a business relationship with you. By the way, if you are the lowest-priced competitor in a certain area, it is still a good idea to understand the nonprice-related reasons that a prospect would decide to buy from you.

Question 15: What do I know about this company?

This is a tricky one, because it is tempting, and wrong, to embark on a full-scale research campaign before you meet with someone for the very first time. I know plenty of successful salespeople whose motto is "I do my research at the first meeting." Even so, however, the truth is that you are competing against people who will take full advantage of easy-to-access information about virtually every company, and it is probably a mistake not to match them, at least in the essentials. This is why it is a good idea to do a little digging to find out every possible piece of information about the company. Visit the company's Web site, and then try to use other internal resources to learn about the prospect's organization. Take just a few minutes to ask other people within your company about sales opportunities that may await you and companies that match up with the one that you are meeting with: Is it like a past customer you sold to? If so, how? If not, can you justify the visit in the first place?

Do not be afraid to call up and cancel an appointment after you learn that the meeting you have set is with someone who is really unlikely to benefit in any way from working with you. If you do decide to show up for the meeting as scheduled, which you probably will, use the research period to identify at least three of your company success stories that you feel are likely to be of interest to this specific prospect. Do not expect to simply recite these stories to the person, however. Become familiar with them and have them ready in case an opportunity to share them comes up.

Question 16: How will I create the flow?

In other words, you want to decide exactly how you are going to open the meeting.

One good opening looks like the following question:

Question 17: Would it help if I told you a little bit about our company and what I do?

Follow up this question by offering a short "commercial" that briefly describes yourself and your company. Again, think in terms of a 30-second discussion on an elevator. This 30-second opening will *not* be an excuse to hold forth with an extensive monologue at the beginning of the meeting. Instead, you should follow your 30-second speech immediately with a question for the other person. Identifying that question, of course, is a critical point in the meeting. And we will talk about identifying that question in the next chapter.

Question 18: What is my Next Step strategy?

You cannot simply walk into a meeting that you have scheduled with a prospect and wait for something interesting to happen. Your goal as a salesperson must be to move the relationship *forward*, and if you are doing your job, you will have both a primary object and a backup strategy in case you do not get exactly what you are after. We will be talking at length about possible Next Steps in Chapters Six and Seven. For now, just remember that before you go to a meeting with any sales leads, you must know what Next Step you will ask for before leaving that first meeting.

By the way, it is estimated that by following this one simple rule—namely, that of asking for the second meeting while you are on the first meeting—you can reduce the length of your sales cycle by between two and four weeks!

The Road Map for a Great Conversation

"Parable selling" means telling a relevant success story about your company. These must be prepared ahead of time.

Now, let's assume you're face-to-face with the prospect for your first meeting. What kinds of questions will help you build rapport? This is, of course, someone you would like to turn into an active prospect. You can only do this by making it easy for the person to decide to work with you, by scheduling your Next Step. Do not open the meeting with a series of predetermined questions! It is very important that you ask questions that will allow the person to open up during the initial phase of the meeting, and failing to ask some variation on the questions you have seen here will shut down the flow of information later on in the conversation. Take your time. Try to connect with this individual as a human being before you start pressuring him or her with questions.

The early portion of the meeting must be used to identify or (if you had a particularly good prospecting call) re-establish something that you have in common with the other person. You might in fact have identified something like that during the initial call, but as your goal is to keep the prospecting call brief and to the point, in most first meetings you probably will not have this information.

You have probably been told by superiors or by the sales "experts" about the importance of building a rapport with someone before launching into the "business" portion of the meeting. This is good advice. However, you do have to be careful *how* you build this rapport. Not long ago, I heard the story of a salesperson who had been carefully coached by her sales manager to say something nice about the prospect's photos of family or friends when she stepped into the person's office. This seemed like a pretty safe bet, considering that just about every cubicle and workspace features some photo of a contact's friends, family, or loved ones. However, this was the new salesperson's first day on the job, and she did not quite have the hang of the rapport-building step yet. She walked into the new contact's office, shook his hand, and looked around the room for the family photos so she could say something nice about them. When she saw the picture on the prospect's desk, she found herself looking at three of the ugliest children she had ever seen in her life.

Without missing a beat, she looked her prospect in the eye, indicated the picture on the desk, smiled, and said, "What a nice frame!"

I think you'll agree that there are better ways to begin a meeting. What is important to remember, above and beyond any questions that you may attempt to ask during this rapport-building phase, is that this initial portion of the meeting must be handled naturally and spontaneously. Stalking into the room and reciting a clearly memorized list of questions designed to "build bridges" with the other person will backfire just as spectacularly as the "what a nice frame" strategy will.

Questions for Building Rapport

The basic principles of developing good rapport-building questions are pretty simple. What follows will allow you to adapt the questions you do ask to virtually any circumstance or person.

1. Construct your rapport-building question around something that both of you can relate to then and there. This means you can feel free to talk about surroundings, the view from the person's window, and so on, if none of the question possibilities presented in this chapter make sense to you.

2. Do not rush the other person, or try to manipulate him or her. If you are trying to open the meeting, and the other person has not said anything yet, or has only made some brief polite remarks, you are not ready to begin the business portion of your meeting.

3. Remember, the sales process unfolds naturally, step-by-step. But it does unfold. You cannot expect to move into the information-gathering stages of the relationship without having established some kind of commonality and rapport. Let the other person set the pace.

4. Understand that there really is a difference between rapport questions and "business" questions. Ask questions in the first category before you begin the "business" portion of the meeting.

These are general guidelines for establishing rapport effectively. Specific questions you can use to build rapport include:

Question 19: How's business?

This is an all-purpose conversation starter that will give you insight, not only into the person's present situation—not only the company's current level of success, but also how your individual contact measures that success. I have more than once met with a CEO who had a hot product or service in an expanding market that his company dominated, but who was nevertheless quite worried about the company's business prospects. My simple question, "How's business?" allows people to share the fact that their business is well positioned for success today, but vulnerable to competitive forces in the future, forces that may be deeply troubling to your contact.

So the simple-sounding question, "How's business?" is a great way to get the other person talking, and also an important tool for measuring both what is happening in this person's world and how he or she interprets and evaluates what is happening.

The following is also an effective question with which to begin the meeting:

Question 20: Can you tell me something I've always wondered—how does someone get an office like this?

This is flattering and effective if you use it with utter sincerity and a twinkle of good humor, but it is obviously only appropriate for situations where you have been privileged to enter a truly impressive personal workspace. If you were to make the mistake of posing this question while seated in a plastic chair in a tiny, dingy cubicle, your contact would probably assume that you were trying to launch a joke at his or her expense.

Your Questioning Strategy

As a general rule, you should avoid any and all "small talk" that points toward politics, religion, sexuality, or other controversial topics. Keep it simple. Keep it clean. And do not fall into the small talk trap. Oftentimes, when salespeople talk too much, the "small talk" period of the meeting has an alienating effect.

Play it safe. Keep the questions focused on the other person's experiences, insights, and choices. Do not get too specific, and do not try to sell anything.

Question 21: Is that your family?

Genuine curiosity and admiration for personal knick-knacks around the office, around the person's workspace—such as a photo of family members—can also serve as effective material for bonding and small talk. Just be careful to follow through appropriately with questions that will help the person feel comfortable about discussing what is happening in his or her family life. If you ask the question, "Is that your family?" and you are greeted with a smile and the answer, "Yes," you might choose to follow through with another question along the following lines: "It looks like your daughter is about high school age, am I right?" This will give the person the opportunity to expand on school activities, what it is like having a teenager in the house, what colleges the daughter is thinking about applying to, etc.

Question 22: How did you become a . . . ?

Or . . .

Question 23: What do you have to study to become a . . . ?

Asking about the person's early career or educational choices is among the safest and most reliable rapport-building strategies. It is very, very difficult to go wrong in the early parts of the meeting with a new person by asking the person what led him or her to the current job. In most cases, you will want to step back and let the person go on a bit about this, because the act of sharing one's history is an important part of the process of bonding with somebody professionally.

Question 24: How long have you been with ABC Company?

This is another way of asking the same basic question, but it has the advantage of pointing you in the direction of the person's recent history with the company. It has a disadvantage, of course, of leaving you staring at an awkward silence if the person has only recently been recruited.

Fortunately, you can always follow up with . . .

Question 25: So how did you come to work here?

Most contacts will be more than happy to fill you in on all the relevant details of how they got the job. Again, the simple act of their sharing this information is just as important as the content of what they pass along. The key in the rapport-building phase is to get the person to open up, to take part in the discussion, and to conclude that it is safe to share information with you.

This question will not work well, of course, if you happen to be meeting with the person who built the company up from nothing over a period of time. For entrepreneurs and other such movers and shakers, you should probably consider a question like . . .

Question 26: How did you decide to take the big step of (launching your company) (going public) (taking on the job of CEO)?

These are the kinds of questions you may want to consider using in an attempt to build rapport with an entrepreneur, CEO, or other high-level decision-maker at a midsize or large company. However, it should be obvious by the nature of the example questions that you have to be careful how you fill in the blanks. If the company does not offer stock publicly, you should not ask how the chief executive came to the decision to go public. This is one of the situations where a little bit of research on the Internet will give you the best insight on how to open the meeting.

YOUR QUESTIONING STRATEGY

One basic, but reliable, rule of thumb should guide your efforts to opening the meeting with senior executives and entrepreneurs: Encourage them to talk about themselves. People who achieve at very high levels and obtain leadership positions within corporate structures tend to be self-focused. That is not a criticism, but simply a fact of life. These individuals like to talk about themselves. So to get started, pose questions about their favorite topic!

Questions for Managing the Transition

When I talked about questions that you need to ask yourself before you go on the first meeting, you were instructed to think about how you would manage the flow into the "business portion" of the meeting. I gave you a brief example of what this would look like. (See Question 17.) Let's look at some variations on this extremely important transitional question in a little more depth.

Once you have made it past the rapport-building phase of the first meeting—a phase that is usually pretty easy to recognize—you will set up the first question of the meeting. It is, as we have seen, a question that will lead you into the information-gathering phase, but it is not focused on generating an in-depth, detailed response from the other person. Instead, it is designed to take the pressure off the other person and allow you to control the flow of the meeting by offering a VERY BRIEF "commercial" about yourself and/or your company, followed by the first "real" question of the meeting.

Question 27: Before we get started, would it help if I told you a little bit about how our company got started?

This is the point in the meeting at which you will pose this question or something like it. Interesting variations include:

Question 28: Would it help if I went first?

If there's a problem, and the other person wants to go first, that's fine. But at least you've initiated the discussion.

Question 29: Would it help if I told you a little bit about the work we did for XYZ Company?

Share a few relevant details about the company you mentioned during your prospecting call, and then ask a question.

Question 30: Would it help if I gave a brief overview of what we usually do during this meeting?

All of these questions and their countless variations are important tools for you to use to establish control of the meeting. Can you see why? The mere fact that you have posed the question determines the subject that you and the other person will be talking about. This is what we mean when we talk about "controlling the flow."

Note that we are not asking the prospect, "What don't you like about the widgets that you are currently using?" We are instead choosing to put the focus on whether or not it would help if we "went first."

This is a very tactful way of establishing our position as the coordinator of the meeting, and of soliciting an initial response from the other person. There is a cliché that prosecuting attorneys will not ask a question to which they do not know the answer. The same is not exactly true for salespeople—we have to ask lots of questions that we do not know the answer to—but we are nevertheless responsible for posing questions and then anticipating where they are going to go. And at this crucial junction in the meeting, we do not want to launch questions that can lead us in a direction with which we are completely unfamiliar.

Control the Flow!

Think of it this way: You really can control the flow of the conversation. You really can control (at least) the starting point of any conversation you initiate with a prospect. If you walk into the room and say, "My goodness. That is the ugliest tie I've ever seen in my life," you can rest assured that the conversation will proceed from that point and no other. By the same token, if you ask the question, "How are you feeling today?" you should not be at all surprised if the person goes on at some length about the state of his or her personal health. After all, that is what you asked about!

To run a meeting effectively, you have to understand this principle of controlling the flow. When you sit down across the desk from a new person, and establish a little bit of rapport with that person, it is in your job description to begin the meeting in such a way that you will able to direct the conversation toward the topics that you feel are most beneficial to the conversation. As a result, you should ask a single question along the lines you have see here, and follow that up immediately with the first substantial question of the discussion.

However, you are going to precede that first substantial question with a question that allows you to say just a little bit about yourself and your company. This is the "thirty-second elevator speech" or "personal commercial" that we talked about earlier. Here is what it might sound like in the form of the dialogue:

> *Me:* So, Mr. Jones, would it help if I told you a little bit about D.E.I. Management Group and what we do?
>
> *Mr. Jones:* Sure.
>
> *Me:* Well I founded D.E.I. in 1979. We're a sales training company that's worked with more than 9,000 companies and trained a half a million people over twenty-five years. Some of

our clients include Aetna, EMC, Imperial Oil, ExxonMobil, and Federal Express. We specialize in training people how to set first appointments, gather the right information, and improve their closing ratios.

(Note that this extremely brief summary of my business has now been completed.)

Me: Just out of curiosity, have you ever worked with a sales training company before? *(This is my first substantial "business" question of the meeting.)*

Do you see how it works? It all unfolds seamlessly . . . but it takes quite a bit of practice to pull off. I call this transition question a "segue" question. It helps you to segue into the first question of the meeting, and it allows you to bridge the gap between the "pleasantry" phase and the "business" phase of the meeting.

Don't Launch into a Monologue!

Use your segue question to pose a very brief commercial or value statement about your company or your own background. DO NOT use it as an excuse to set up a long-winded lecture about every single aspect of your private service. DO NOT try to sell to the other person. Remember, this is a thirty-second transition into the first "real" question of the meeting.

I hope you will forgive me if I am restating key points here, but they are points that are so frequently neglected that they are worth emphasizing. If you were to take 100 salespeople at random, and monitor the first five minutes of their first meeting with a new contact, you would, I think, find all four of the following problems in ninety of those cases:

■ Faulty or nonexistent establishment of rapport

- Faulty or nonexistent attempts to establish strategic control of the flow of conversation
- Faulty or nonexistent initial questioning followed by . . .
- Extended monologues about a specific application of the salesperson's product or service, or about the history of the company the salesperson works for

Don't make these mistakes during your meeting!

In order to improve your closing ratio, you must set a higher standard. Lay the groundwork for gathering information more efficiently. Resist the temptation to "share everything" during the rapport-building phase. You will only alienate your contact if you do.

Chapter Three

Opening Questions to Figure Out What the Person and the Company Do

You should spend most of your time in the sales process gathering information about what the other person does, and the questions in this chapter and the next are your best tools for doing just that.

Two Kinds of Questions

There are two main categories for the questions you should be prepared to ask once you have initiated contact and developed a little rapport:

- Your first "business" question
- Everything else

In this chapter, you will be looking at some candidates for the question you can use as the first "business" question of the meeting.

(Note: All of the possible "first" questions you are about to read can also be effective queries for later on in the discussion, of course. I'm separating them because it's very important to select—and practice—the question with which you intend to open the meeting.)

The First Question

At the end of your brief thirty-second summary, you are going to ask a fateful question: the first real question of your meeting. It is quite possible that this question will be the "knockout" question you saw as Question 10 in this book. (In my own industry of sales training, you'll recall, that the knockout question sounds like this: "How many salespeople do you have?")

If, however, you have already identified the answers to the knockout question and you know that this is, in fact, a good person or organization for you to talk to, you will want to identify the opening question that you plan to use with great care, and you will want to do that long before you walk in the door.

I cannot tell you what the right opening question for your next meeting should be. I can only tell you that it is vitally important for you to choose it carefully.

The right opening question will vary from meeting to meeting and from contact to contact. There is, alas, no single opening question that will deliver the right information in every situation. The following questions are just some of the possibilities to choose from.

Question 31: I checked our records, and I noticed that you are not working with us. Why not?

Not too long ago, I had a meeting with a young man, who was attempting to sell me advertising in the Yellow Pages. His initial question to me was "What don't you like about your current advertising?" That is a very common opening question, and it is totally ineffective. It focuses on the need, the pain, the problem—all those things that I warned you about as being superficial and even a little off-putting to the prospect. A better opening question for him might have been one modeled after Question 31.

This is, in fact, the question that that Yellow Pages sales representative should have asked me. Instead of focusing on what "pain" I was experiencing with my current advertiser, he should have opened up his own copy of the Yellow Pages, looked for my company's name, noticed that it was not there, and asked me why I was not already in the Yellow Pages. If he had done this, we could have had a much more meaningful conversation about what my advertising goals were—or were not. But as it happened, all he did was ask me what pain I was feeling. I told him I was not feeling any pain or discomfort, and I ended the meeting.

Look at the question again. Think about how you might adapt it to your situation.

Question 32: I am just curious. Have you ever worked with a company like ours before?

This is an effective variation on Question 31 if you are hesitant about demanding why the person is not working with you now, or if you feel that somehow is coming on too strongly.

I freely admit that the question as I have phrased it in #31 can be a little tricky if your company is not a major player or does not have some kind of previous association with the person to whom you are speaking. I should tell you, however, that a variation on this question that I helped an affiliate telephone representative come up with resulted in a huge order from the very first person with whom he met. He sat down across from his prospect and asked, "I noticed you are not working with our company for your cellular service—why not?" And waited to see what would happen next. What happened next is that he ended up having an in-depth discussion with his contact about the organization's communication priorities and the working relationship it had with the last vendor—and he secured a major new account from that meeting!

Whether you try the advanced version or this beginner's version, this kind of question is an excellent way to begin your first meeting with a contact, and may be right for you.

Why You Can't Use the Same Opening Question for Every Meeting

You have now seen two variations on a good question you can use to open your initial meeting with a prospect. The problem is that even a good question like "I checked my records and I noticed that you are not working with us. . . . I'm just curious, why not?"—cannot and *should* not be used every time you get together with someone. Here are the three big reasons.

1. No opening question is going to be appropriate to every sales situation. So if you use the same question at the opening of every discussion, it's either going to be off-base or so vague as to be meaningless.
2. Asking the same opening question all the time makes it more difficult for you to remember the answer the person gives you. You'll be more likely to confuse this person's answer with the last person's answer.
3. Asking the same opening question all the time means

falling into a curiosity-destroying routine. The less curious you are, the worse your interviews will be.

Salespeople live and die by routine, and that is both a blessing and a curse. It is a blessing because the routine instills discipline in the salesperson's life, and provides a reliable series of benchmarks and activities that one can follow over time and use to deliver a predictable result. The downside of routine, however, is that we may fall into the trap of running every meeting exactly the same way, and losing sight of the fact that the individual we are talking to really is an individual.

Question 33: What made you want to consider (widgets)?

Not long ago I had the pleasure of taking a call from someone who had decided that he wanted to contact our company to deliver sales training to his organization. This is one of these "dream calls"—the kind of call where the person says, "I have 150 salespeople and I would like you to come in and train them. I read your book, I love what you guys do, and I am ready to set up training. What do you charge?"

Now, twenty years ago, I would have taken that call and started in asking about timing, pricing and what kind of schedule for the day the prospect was trying to set up. But nowadays, I handle this kind of call a bit differently. Here is what I said: *"That's great. Thanks for calling. Just out of curiosity, what made you decide that you wanted to invest in sales training for people?"*

For a lot of people, a question like this is a little scary. They assume that the sale is closed, and that asking questions about motive or decision will only increase the likelihood of losing the deal. But actually, just the opposite is true.

Why This Question Is So Important

Think about it. This person did not decide to call me up and try to book a sales training date for his staff because he did not have anything better to do on a Tuesday afternoon. He called me because *something had changed* in his world. Now, at least from the tone of the initial call, it sounds as though he has decided to sign on with us. That may or may not be true. (I've had plenty of these kinds of calls turn out to be dead ends.) But even if it is true, it is definitely in my best interest to find out what has changed in this person's world before I start booking the training date.

Why? Because my goal is to get people to *use* what I offer . . . not just today, but forever. When I establish a professional training relationship with one of my clients, I do not want to be there for just a week, I want that person to build me into the orientation process for every salesperson who comes on staff, from now until the end of time. (Okay, that's a slight exaggeration. But you get the idea.)

And by the way, there is another very good reason for me to try to identify exactly what has changed in this person's world and to get a better sense of what prompted him to pick up the telephone and call me. Even though it sounds as though he has made up his mind, the hard truth of the matter is that my relationship with this person is only about forty-five seconds old. It is entirely possible that this person is calling *five or six* training companies, saying precisely the same thing to all, and evaluating their offerings before picking a single vendor. Mind you, I don't say that I know that this is what is happening, but I do say it is a possibility. That is why I want to gather more information and have more back and forth with the person before I make any kind of commitment.

By asking the person who called "ready to buy" precisely what made him decide that he wanted to invest in sales training for his salespeople, I was able to identify some very interesting information. First and foremost, he wanted to retain his highest performing salespeople. That is a different objective than wanting to recruit good salespeople in the first place, and it is one that I needed to know in order to build the right program for him. Second, I learned that he was interested in improving the prospecting skills of his least experienced salespeople, but that he had no such concerns when it came to his senior people. Once again, this allowed me to position my program correctly.

YOUR QUESTIONING STRATEGY

The more information you uncover, the better the relationship gets . . . and the more *reliable* the information gets. Often in sales, we uncover a fact at the end of the conversation that should have come up at the beginning. Or we uncover a fact during the second meeting that was glossed over or misrepresented during the first meeting. People tend to share more accurate information with people whom they trust than with people whom they do not know very well. Be sure to factor this in when you are with a prospect.

After about fifteen minutes of conversation on the phone—during which he did most of the talking—we were able to come to an understanding of the main point of the sales training program that I would be presenting to him when we got together in person. That is the outcome of the call that I wanted—a face-to-face meeting—and that is the outcome I got. Notice that I was able to take the initiative and learn some critical information about what this particular prospect was trying to accomplish by asking this question: *What made you decide you wanted sales training?*

This is an excellent question to use when you inherit a "hot" lead, someone who has expressed a genuine interest in working with you or your company, or has even told you he or she is actively in the marketplace evaluating a number of vendors. If you do not know what the person's thought process is, how he or she got to the point where they said "we need X," then you will be missing key information. You will be tempted to pass along "boilerplate" recommendations that worked for the last prospect, but might not necessarily be right for this one. Such a proposal may work to close this deal, but it will not get you much closer to the goal of ensuring that the person works with you forever.

Question 34: Have you ever reached out to a company like ours before? If so, who was it? Why them?

Obviously, this is a variation on the "I checked my records and I notice you're not working with us" question. With this version, you will be able to get a sense of whether the person has ever considered investing in products or services like yours. You should only use this question when you are relatively certain that the prospect is not currently using something, a product or service, of the kind that you offer.

Question 35: Mr. Jones, my guess is that you are an XYZ customer. What made you choose them?

This is an excellent opening question for those situations where you know, or have a strong instinct, that the customer is using one of your competitors.

If you walk in the door, see your competition's logo everywhere, and see framed copies of letters to your contact from your competition's president, you might as well get to the heart of the matter. Manage the small-talk portion coming in, ask your "segue question," deliver your 30-second commercial, and then get down to business. Ask the contact specifically what made him or her choose to work with ABC Company.

Question 36: How did you choose ABC?

For use in the same situation. This is much more effective than asking the person whether he was "involved" in the decision to select that vendor. Think about it. It's extremely rare that you run into somebody on a first meeting who will volunteer that he or she had no real role in selecting a vendor.

YOUR QUESTIONING STRATEGY

Very often, people will inflate the role that they played in selecting a vendor, to make it clear that they are important people within the organization. But if the person has no knowledge whatsoever about the standards used to select the vendor in question, you can rest assured he or she was not involved in the decision—and you will have to find some way to connect with other people in the company!

Question 37: What is the main thing that you are trying to accomplish this month/quarter/year?

This is an opening you can use in a situation where you really do not have a lot of information to work with. It is the kind of question that will, with any luck, give you insights into precisely what your contact envisions, what he or she is responsible for making happen, and perhaps even an early glimpse about how you might fit into the overall picture.

A good variation on this, for use in those situations when

you know that your contact is facing a commitment to turn somebody else's vision into a concrete reality, looks like this:

Question 38: What is the main thing that your CEO/president/boss is trying to accomplish this month/quarter/year?

There are only two situations where this question is *not* a great way to start a meeting. They are 1) the situation where you have no idea who the person's superior is, and 2) the situation where you are talking to the founder or president of the company.

You will encounter any number of people for whom success is determined by their ability to keep a higher-up happy. This is a question to share with such a person. Your goal is to make it clear that you are as focused on keeping the boss happy as he or she is, and you are willing to take notes on, and execute, his or her interpretation of what the boss wants. In a perfect world, of course, you would like to be able to work your way up to meet face-to-face with the boss whose aims the contact is assessing, but that is not always possible. Use this question and intelligent follow-ups to it to identify precisely what this person thinks is on the top banana's agenda. Be sure to specify a particular time period, because an open-ended question like this may lead to long monologues about vision, value statements, and corporate philosophies. These are interesting, but not necessarily what you are after in terms of developing a timeline to work together.

Question 39: What kind of person is your CEO?

You should only use this question in situations where you already know at least a little bit about the CEO in question.

Question 40: What made you decide to call us?

This is a variation on the "What made you decide on widgets?" question. Obviously, this question is limited to situations in which the prospect has contacted you or otherwise found a way to reach out to you. This is a question that can be adapted with very good results to the world of telesales: If you happen to be selling in an inbound telesales environment; that means, you spend most of your day receiving calls from people who have contacted you in response to a mailing, circular, Internet offer, advertising campaign, or other promotional device.

However, the marketing strategy used to generate the call is only a surface reflection of the information you really need: namely, what it is that has changed in a person's world. If nothing has changed for this person, you can rest assured that he or she would not have picked up the telephone to call your company. The same principle applies to situations where we are meeting with someone who has contacted us and asked for a face-to-face discussion. There is really not much point in trying to gather information about anything else until we have learned what motivated the person to reach out to us. After all, the person did not go to the trouble of contacting us because there was nothing better to do that morning!

Question 41: What were you going to do about your (widget) problem if I had not called you?

This is an excellent question to ask at the beginning of a meeting with a person whom you know to be "in the marketplace"—that is, searching for potential vendors or otherwise making a conscious effort to address a clearly identified problem. If you know the person is trying to resolve a challenge that you know you can have some positive impact in addressing, it really is to your advantage to find out what the current plan is.

Question 42: Just out of curiosity, whom do you consider to be your important competition?

The prospect's answer to this question will give you important insight into what is going on in the person's industry, how the company is doing, and the priorities and duties of the person with whom you have hooked up.

Question 43: How do you think you stack up against the competition?

Do not be afraid to ask a decision-maker within the organization how he or she feels the organization stacks up against the competition. A fair number of senior executives seem to make a lifetime commitment to the job of identifying areas where the competition is outperforming them, analyzing ways to combat this and all the possible strategies for overcoming the performance gap identified. Someone who takes this approach to the question is very likely to be a person of authority or a person "on the way up." By the same token, a person who is complacent about the competition and who believes that it represents no real threat to his or her employer's operations is unlikely to hold a position of great practical authority and influence within the company.

Note that I am not suggesting that every key decision-maker will have a cynical or pessimistic answer to this question; only that these people will be more likely to take a realistic look at the challenges they face from the outside. These decision-makers are also willing to share what they feel to be their company's competitive advantages with you, but they must, by definition, develop some sense of what is working and what is not for their competitors in the marketplace.

Even significant market share is not any guarantee of dominance of a given market, and most successful executives know this. That is why this question, and intelligent follow-ups to it, can be such an eye-opening experience for a salesperson eager to identify the priorities of the movers and shakers within the organization.

Question 44: How do you distinguish yourself in an industry like this?

Interesting variations on this important question include:

Question 45: How do you maintain a competitive edge in an industry as tough as this one?

And . . .

Question 46: How do you set yourself apart from your competition?

The way you form the question really depends on your personal preference and the initial research that you have done on the company.

What you dig up about the company and the competition is nowhere near as important—or interesting—as what your contact and his or her peers within the target company have decided regarding their own competitive position. How are they reaching out to customers? What is their value proposition?

Is the company experiencing growth or decline in market share? How big is the industry? How big a player are they within it? Where does the CEO see them going?

If this question elicits some kind of story about the organization's mission, you can rest assured that the odds are very good that you are not talking to a true decision-maker. Try to escalate the sale in such a way as to get exposure to someone who knows exactly how the target company stacked up against the competition. (You will find strategies for doing just this later on in the book.)

Question 47: What are you doing right now to . . . ?

The opening question of your meeting, as we have seen, will help to determine the flow of the entire conversation. It is hard to imagine a better opening discussion than one that arises naturally from this query . . . as long as you complete it correctly!

If you are selling telecom services, the question should sound like this:

Question 48: What are you doing right now to control your telecom costs and to keep people connected?

Notice how the way that this question *concludes* focuses on an area where we know we are able to add value. We do not walk in the door and say to the person, "What are you doing right now to earn extra points on your calling card program?" The person to whom we are speaking may not have a calling card program and may not earn any extra points. That is an example of a question that is built around our preconceptions and understandings of the prospect's situation, which are often erroneous.

Nor do we pose the question this way: "What are you doing right now to maximize usage of your long-distance carrier's network resources?"

This is an example of the question that simply demands too much technical knowledge of the other person. Unless you are dealing with a very analytical or technically driven person, it is quite likely this question will lead you to a one- or two-word response. Certainly, if you are face-to-face with an executive whose day is built around making interesting things happen, you should not begin your meeting by focusing on technical questions to which he or she probably does not know the answer.

Let's take another example. Let's suppose you are selling training services. If you are to ask this question, you could compose it a number of different ways and uncover interesting information that will give you an insight into the prospect's world. Examples include:

Question 49: What are you doing right now to train your salespeople?

Or . . .

Question 50: What are you doing right now to retain your key people?

Or . . .

Question 51: What are you doing right now for employee orientation?

Or . . .

Question 52: What are you doing right now to deal with the competitive pressures that your salespeople face in this industry?

Notice that each of the questions focuses on an area where we know we can add value. Notice also, that each of these questions gives the other person an easy point of entry into the conversation. We would *not* want to ask: "What are you doing right now to increase your employee's overall performance on standardized post-training testing?" This is a narrowly focused, overly analytical question that is entirely from the point of view of the person making the sale, not from the person who will derive a benefit from working with us.

Finally, here is another example of how to use this classic, and extremely effective, opening question. Let's say you are working in the importing and exporting industry. A good opening question might be:

Question 53: What are you doing right now to track and manage your overseas shipments?

Notice that in this question, we have specified tracking and managing as something we want to find out more about. This would be a pretty good idea if we know that part of the reason people ultimately decide to work with us is that we offer superior tracking and management resources.

There are any number of good ways to open a meeting, but an intelligent variation on the "What are you doing right now to . . ." question is probably among the best. If you pose it at the right time, with the right focus, and to the right person, you really will get important insight on how likely it is that you may be able to build value on both sides by working with this person.

Notice, however, that if the person with whom you are speaking has no idea what the company is doing in an area where you believe you may be able to add value to the organization, it is very likely that you are talking to the wrong person! Later in the book, I'll give you some ideas on how to move and expand your network within the organization to find the right contact.

Question 54: Just so I know where we are headed, what is the main thing you want your vendor to accomplish here?

Here is a variation on "What are you trying to accomplish?" that puts the spotlight on the vendor. This question is an excellent starting point for a meeting with a decision-maker with a contact whose motives, experience, and role in the organization are basically unknown to you. You will learn a lot from the response you get, both about this person's priorities, and his or her level of goal orientation.

If you have scheduled a meeting with a midlevel functionary who has no real authority, it is unlikely that you will get a great deal of information about the organization's initiatives or priorities, but rather a full rundown on the process by which this person gets through the day and the rules and regulations under which the organization operates. If you do find yourself face-to-face with such a person on the first meeting, you will want to find a way to escalate the sale in such a way to gain access to the real decision-maker.

The Power of the Right Question
Not long ago, I closed a major deal for our organization with the lowest of low-tech approaches, and in a setting where all of my competitors were armed with laptops, charts, PowerPoint presentations, standup displays, and various other

snazzy-looking sales tools. I was the last potential vendor to make my way into the conference room that day, and I could tell from the looks on the faces of the people in that conference room that they had had just about enough of flashy presentations and multicolored graphics. I passed out my business cards, shook hands, pulled out my yellow legal pad, and got right to the point. I asked, "Tell me something—what is the main thing you guys are trying to accomplish in your next sales training program?"

The president of the company, who had been gazing into the distance philosophically, suddenly snapped to life, met my gaze, and smiled. "You know," he said, "you are the very first person to ask us that question today."

I got the training deal for our company. To this day, I remain convinced that we got that business because I was the only one in the group willing to focus on the prospect's agenda for the meeting, rather than my own.

Question 55: What were your goals for today's meeting?

This is a question you should use only in very clearly identified circumstances. Ask this question at the outset of a meeting when you know for a fact that the person you are dealing with is a senior executive.

In this situation—which arises fairly frequently among salespeople who are energetic about broadcasting their company's results to the world at large, and who receive a great deal of positive word of mouth—you really want to identify what the other person's agenda is before attempting to proceed with anything substantial in a meeting.

On the other hand, if you yourself have initiated the contact, it is very unlikely that this question will generate much interest. If you have made a good effort to schedule the first appointment, and then showed up face-to-face with the implied promise of some spectacular program or product that you want to discuss, it is probably not a great idea to ask the other person what the goals of the meeting should be. This is your meeting. You called it. You should be running it.

Question 56: How do you plan to . . . ?

This question, a variation on the "What are you doing now to . . . " question, can be used either as the initial "business" question, or as the first follow-up question, but it is absolutely imperative that you find someway to pose it during the first meeting. So please make a note here to build this seemingly open-ended question into your interviewing routine.

Missing the Point

A while ago, I met with a representative from a major investment bank who stepped into my office, shook my hand, sat down, and began to share his lengthy monologue about why his company was the best investment operation around. About five minutes into this, I stopped him.

"Wait a minute," I said. "Did you even look at this office?"

He stopped short.

He looked around the office.

"It's a very nice office," he said.

"Thanks," I said. "Have you met with a lot of people who have offices that are nice like this?"

"Some," he said, as he shifted around in his chair uneasily.

"What does someone having a nice office mean to you?" I asked.

"I don't understand," he said.

"What's my job title?" I asked.

"I think you're the president of the company, right?"

"That's right," I said. "So, I'm the president of the company, I have a nice office, and it's as nice as a lot of the other people you've met with. What should that tell you about me?"

He thought for a moment.

"That you're important?"

"Nope," I said. "What it really should tell you is that the odds are very good that *I already have some kind of investment plan.*"

"Yeah," he smiled and shook his head. "Good point," he said. "I guess you would."

"So, if I already have an investment plan," I continued, "just like most of the other people you've met with, wouldn't you want to know what that plan is?"

"Yeah, I guess I would."

"Do you ever ask the people you meet with about what their current investment plan is?"

"Um . . . not yet."

"Don't you think that would be a good way to start the meeting?"

"Sure."

"So, why don't you ask that?"

"Have you already got some kind of investment plan in place?" he asked.

"I sure do," I said.

He didn't get my business—I'm sure that's not a surprise to you—but he could have done a better job of building rapport at the beginning of the meeting by asking me what my current plan was.

Let's look at another example. Say you're selling advertising on the World Wide Web—advertising that is designed to help companies to attract potential franchisees—people who will decide to purchase a territory and a business system from a parent company. If you are meeting with someone, or speaking to someone on the phone, about how you might be able to work with his or her company, you would eventually want to ask this:

Question 57: How do you plan to reach out to (prospective franchisees)?

The focus is on the person's plan for the future. Note the disadvantages of phrasing the question in this way:

How are you planning to use the World Wide Web?

Look how much more effective the other approach is. It focuses on what the perspective customer is planning to do, namely how he will be attracting new franchisees who will pay *X* thousand dollars for the right to set up business in a certain geographical territory and employ the company's business system.

Or suppose that you sell those insulated windows that are designed to keep energy bills down and increase the efficiency of home heating and cooling systems. During the initial conversation with your prospect, you would want to consider asking the following:

Question 58: What is your plan for (cutting down on your heating bill costs this winter—have you thought about that at all)?

If there is a plan, you'll find out what it is. Of course, you could also have asked . . .

Question 59: What are you doing right now to keep (your heating costs down)?

Both of these questions will focus on the key concern of the homeowner, which is to avoid having to spend large amounts of money to heat the home during the cold winter months. (If you are reading this in sunny California or tropical Hawaii, you will just have to use your imagination for this section, and take it on faith that there are, in fact, dreadful winters to be endured in the northern United States.)

Here is a third example. Let us say your job is to sell those self-service coffee machines to small and midsize offices. You know the kind I mean: the self-service units that allow you to brew a fresh cup of coffee every time you want one, one cup at a time. The company rents the machines, and sells the supplies to businesses that do not have cafeteria or café facilities onsite.

Suppose you're meeting someone who's planning to open a new branch office in your territory. At some point in the initial discussion, you will definitely want to ask your prospect:

Question 60: What is your plan for (providing coffee service for your employees)?

This question will allow you to identify exactly what is going on in the prospect's world and determine how the firm plans to get employees access to coffee during the course of the day. By asking it, and following up intelligently, you will be able to help your prospect focus on the potential lost man-hours associated with running down the block to the nearest coffee shop, or the potential safety hazards of keeping a standard coffee maker on the "warm" setting for twelve or fourteen hours at a time—not to mention the potential problems if someone forgets to turn the machine off!

What you would want to avoid, however, is posing the question this way: *Are you finally tired of wasting money on your coffee service?*

This is insultingly one-dimensional and it assumes your prospect is not bright enough to have made a change before this point.

Let us look at one last example that will illustrate how to pose this extremely important question. Remember, our goal is to focus on the potential benefit that we know we can deliver, not on the "process" or "feature" of what we sell. Suppose that your job is to sell end-of-year gifts for employees, and other rewards designed to serve as an incentive for key people in the organization. You have probably seen these products yourself if you have worked at any midsize company for longer than a year. Somewhere near the middle of December, you may have received a gift from your boss, or perhaps a catalog that shows employees a number of gifts from which to choose at the company's expense. The gifts might be a cordless phone, a DVD player and home theater system, a food processor, or any number of other similar items. Companies set up these gifts and award programs and sell them to senior decision-makers and managers within their market. So, assuming that you are a salesperson for this company, what would your variation on this question look like? To my way of thinking, it should go something like this:

Question 61: What are you planning to do to (retain your key people)?

By identifying what is happening in the area where you wish to add value, and by focusing on the goal of your prospect, namely to hold on or to offer incentives to key people, you are very likely to get a decent picture of precisely what is going on within the prospective account in this area. You would want to avoid asking a question like the following:

What did you give your employees last year at holiday time?

Can you see the problem you face in posing this kind of question? The company may not have "given" the employees anything, at least not any product or premium. It may instead have focused on a cash incentive program, or on days off, or on public recognition at some special awards ceremony. But you would not find out about any of those things unless you asked how the company was currently developing incentives to retain and motivate its key people.

I have devoted a good deal of attention to variations on these particular kinds of "do" questions. They can give us insights into exactly what the prospect is undertaking right now in the area of most interest to us. The key is to spend the time necessary to identify exactly what it is that we sell that will add value from the other person's point of view. Once we do that, we can build the second half of this question so that it is uniquely appropriate to our selling environment.

Question 62: If I worked here, how would I get started and what would my first week look like?

This is an excellent opening question, one that can help you get the other person to open up and also make it clear that you're focusing on something other than the short-term sale. If you don't know what the employers at your target organization are facing, what sort of people they recruit, what sort of obstacles they must overcome, and what kind of training they received, you really don't know much about the company. Be sure to follow up with appropriate "how" and "why" questions.

It's precisely this type of question that can help build a

bond with a prospect that encourages him to share steadily more meaningful "insider intelligence" with us. If we focus only on questions directly related to our product or service, we won't really find out much about what the organization does . . . and we won't learn anything meaningful about what life is like for those who work within the firm.

Question 63: My guess is, your people face challenge (*X*). What do you think?

This is an extremely important question, but one that must be used with great skill and followed up appropriately (see the next question).

This question is only to be used in those situations where you really feel that your product or service can add value to the person's operation. The fact that you've reached this conclusion is interesting, but it's really not as relevant as what your prospect has concluded. Instead of doing what most salespeople do—namely, proclaim that we have the solution and start reciting a memorized speech about it—we're going to ask a question that very subtly introduces our interpretation of the situation, and then asks for the prospect input and endorsement before we proceed any further.

Using This Question as Part of a Longer Sequence

Please note that Question 63 is the first question in an important sequence of questions. Here's what it looks like in the sales training industry.

I first say, "My guess is that your people have plateaued here. My sense, based on what you've said so far today, is that they've been with the company for a while. They don't have any problem hitting a certain minimal level of performance, but that they really aren't moving much beyond that. What do you think?"

Note that this is not me making a diagnosis so much as offering a series of observations and then immediately requesting input from the other person. When I ask, "What do you think?" it's a pretty good bet I will get some kind of agreement. If the person feels radically different about the situation than I do, of course I'll want to know about that, too. But I'm an expert in my field, and the reason that they're talking to me, at least most of the time, is to get my take on the situation. So, when I say something like this—"My guess is that your people have plateaued"—the person is likely to agree. Once they do, I will ask . . .

Question 64: Why do you think that's happening?

This is the all-important follow-through question to Question 63. Notice that before I supply any explanations of the facts that the prospect and I agree are before us, I am going to give him or her a chance to interpret and explain the situation. Nine times out of ten, however, the person *won't* have meaningful input. There may be a stock response, but in fact they know full well that I work with a lot of sales teams, and so they'll turn to me and say, "Well, I think it might be a number of things, but I'm most interested in your take on this. Why do *you* think it's happening?"

It's at that point that I'll go into a much more detailed overview of what my company offers. I'll say something like this: "My guess is that they're not prospecting enough, and that the basic daily activities really haven't been built into their routine. My feeling is that they're probably just coasting on referrals from existing accounts, and that they could go to the next level if they just did a little bit more prospecting and made that a regular habit."

Note what I've done here. What you just read is exactly what I wanted to say, probably from within about five minutes of shaking hands with the prospect. It's entirely possible that I would have had an initial fix on what the situation in that person's sales staff is right off the bat, after just a few questions. But even though I have the feeling that I "know what's going on," I can't simply lead the meeting with my recommendation. I must both establish rapport with the individual, open lines of communication, *and get his or her take on what's going on.* Then, and only then, can I start to give an initial sense of where I think the problem may be.

To offer an example of how this very important question sequence works, I've used my own industry. But the same strategy can apply to virtually any field of endeavor, and I think you'll find it very easy to insert the specifics of your own sales environment. Follow the same sequence, and make sure you get the other person's input before you launch a brief overview of what you think might be the matter. This is a question sequence that should be saved for some point in the second half of your face-to-face meeting.

Question 65: Sometimes people have a problem with (*X*). What's your take on that?

Let's say you've established a little rapport, but you still feel you haven't quite connected with your prospect. This is a good query for the prospect who is having difficulties opening up to you—not because of any lack of conversational material, perhaps, but because he or she simply is not a good conversationalist.

Use a question like this to help guide the person into a

meaningful area of discourse. Don't try to use the question to "shoehorn" the prospect into agreeing to something or making a commitment for which he or she is not ready. Simply pick an area of mutual interest, some place where it's possible that you could deliver value, and ask a broad-based question that references what other people in the industry have told you.

Question 66: Other people in your industry have told me (X). Is that your experience?

This is an interesting variation on the "some people have had a problem with . . ." question. Consider using it when the prospect seems unfamiliar with your company or experience, and be prepared to say which people shared the observation with you. You should also be ready to share relevant success stories that involve the people you reference. (Ideally, you should be willing and able to pass along the person's contact information so your prospect can call the person up directly.)

In this chapter, you have seen a few examples of effective questions you can use to open your meeting. It is important to understand that the first "real" question you ask during your initial contact with a prospect is an extremely important moment in the relationship, if only because it will help you to establish the flow of everything that follows from that point forward. It should go without saying that if your own research or experience indicates some unique new area that you should build a question around, by all means feel free to develop a new question. Just remember that the goal of the opening question is not only to identify some critical piece of information, but also to encourage the other person to share his or her story and insights with you.

Chapter Four

Follow-Through Questions to Figure Out What the Person and the Company Do

I t takes time and practice to become good at asking effective follow-through questions in a sales setting. Here are some basic points to bear in mind.

- Asking effective follow-through questions means being able to focus on the challenges of the other person, not on what you are trying to accomplish.
- Asking effective follow-through questions means being able to anticipate the kinds of business challenges that directly affect the company.

■ Asking effective follow-through questions will help you accelerate your sales cycle and deepen your relationship. It will also increase levels of customer satisfaction.

■ Asking effective follow-through questions means doing more than "just listening." It means being an intelligent interviewer.

It follows that you should . . .

1. Be genuinely interested about how a business works and why people in an organization do things in the way that they do. If you do not have a natural curiosity about how businesses operate, you are not in the right line of business!

2. Be willing to ask yourself: How does this company make money? Who are the customers? What kinds of competitive challenges do the company and the individual contact face in seeking out profit? These are the kinds of questions you must be willing to pose to your contact; it is also good practice to ask the same questions of your own company and the key decision-makers within it.

3. Ask questions about the organization. If you are not curious about how the organization is structured, who its key suppliers and customers are, and what it is doing to extend its reach or maintain its market share, again, you are in the wrong line of work.

4. Ask questions about how the contact's job fits in with the organization's objectives. It is not enough to know about either one in the abstract—you must be willing to ask from both directions. If you have a good understanding of the other person's job, you will have a good understanding of the way the company operates as well. Think of them as halves of a whole.

5. Ask questions about words or ideas that do not make

sense to you. There is an interesting double standard at work here. As a salesperson, you must expect, as a matter of course, to be exposed to a great deal of internal jargon or industry terminology that makes sense intuitively to your prospect, but is not at all clear to you. If you fail to ask for clarification on what these terms mean, you are not effectively performing your job! By the same token, however, you must make every effort to ensure that your own industry's jargon and terminology are made abundantly clear for your prospect. Don't be afraid of "looking dumb." Ask the question.

YOUR QUESTIONING STRATEGY

It is not the prospect's job to volunteer information about your organization's terminology. It *is* your job to clarify any potentially unfamiliar terms for the benefit of your prospect. Too many salespeople follow the principle that the more highfalutin words and technobabble they use, the more they are impressing the other person with their level of knowledge and expertise. Nothing could be further from the truth.

Your job is to gather information and relate it to your company's skill and resource capacity. If you do not know what the other person is talking about, it is very difficult to do that.

The 80/20 Rule of Sales Conversations

A classic sales rule has it that 80 percent of your income typically comes from 20 percent of your customers. A rule of thumb for conducting an effective sales interview uses the same two figures.

During a good sales meeting, a salesperson should be doing only 20 percent of the talking, and the prospects should be doing the remaining 80 percent. As often repeated as that advice is, the fact remains that very few salespeople actually pass this test during the course of their initial meeting with a prospect. The reason for this is actually very simple: When we find ourselves in periods of high stress, we tend to rely on that which we know best. Certainly, meeting with a prospect for the first time can be classified, for many people, as a stressful situation.

So what happens? We fall back on what we know best, and that is our product or service. We spend the majority of the meeting "walking the contact through" the product brochure or a memorized summary of all the features of the product or service. The person on the other side of the desk may be nodding and smiling, but there is no exchange of meaningful information in these kinds of discussions.

The questions in this chapter and the previous one, however, will lead you in a very different direction. If you take a moment to look back at the questions I have given as good examples of queries for the opening of the "business portion" of the meeting, you will see that they are all designed to encourage the other person to open up. If you pose these questions, and follow up on them effectively, you will be much more likely to follow the elusive 80/20 rule for a sales interview.

What Is an Effective Follow-Through Question?

An effective follow-up question is basically any question that encourages the other person to share a *story* about his or her business challenges. Human beings communicate through stories. We share them with each other to illustrate lessons we have learned, mistakes we have made, goals we have set for ourselves and our companies, and the criteria we use to establish our most important business relationships. So that is a very simple yardstick of whether or not you have asked an effective follow-through question: whether or not it encourages a person to tell you the story about his or her world.

Follow-through questions that encourage other people to share stories with us tend to focus on the following elements:

■ **The past**—What happened before the event, decision, or circumstance the person is sharing with you? What situations did he or she inherit? What long-term friend was there for him or her to deal with?

■ **The present**—Who is currently working on the initiative your contact is talking about? How are the current initiatives being measured? What current steps are being taken to establish organizational change, or to ensure that the status quo is maintained?

■ **The future**—What trends does the person, or the organization, foresee having to deal with in the long term? What competitive challenges are on the horizon? What new opportunities must be pursued within the next month, year, or quarter, that are not being pursued right now?

■ **How?**—For every past, present, or future question, what specific methods were used, are being used, or will be used?

■ **Why?**—For every past, present, or future question, what are the current reasons for doing what is being done now? What motors will drive future initiatives?

Before we look at the specific questions you may wish to build the rest of the first meeting around, I would like to warn you not to treat this as some kind of "checklist" exercise. Here's what an effective follow-through question sequence looks like:

Your initial "business" question, and then . . .

Spontaneous follow-up question based on specific response A
Spontaneous follow-up question based on specific response B
Spontaneous follow-up question based on specific response C

Your second "business" question, and then . . .

Spontaneous follow-up question based on specific response A
Spontaneous follow-up question based on specific response B
Spontaneous follow-up question based on specific response C

And so on. It *does not* look like this:

Your initial question, and then . . .

Predetermined follow-up question A
Predetermined follow-up question B
Predetermined follow-up question C
Predetermined follow-up question D
Predetermined follow-up question E

And so on, *ad infinitum.*

In other words, you cannot walk in the door knowing fifty questions that you plan to ask and then pursuing each of them in order. That is not a sales interview, but rather an interrogation similar to the "interviews" that telephone opinion poll surveys conduct.

Your goal is to raise a large issue, examine each of the relevant issues raised by the prospect's response, explore that issue fully, and then move on to the next "big question." After posing your second "big question," you will explore all the ramifications of that question, and so forth. This is a less predictable, but much more effective, means of gathering information from your prospects than simply working your way through a prede-termined list of questions.

YOUR QUESTIONING STRATEGY

Think of the five or six major issues that you want to cover in the meeting, and be sure to explore all the ramifications of each one.

What's the alternative? Subjecting your prospect to a battery of questions you have memorized but he or she has not? This destroys any rapport you have built up and tends to make people feel that they are on the spot. Even if the person is unfazed by the intensity, you may be so eager to move on to the next question that you neglect the implications of something important that your prospect has just said!

Question 67: "So—are you currently . . . ?" (the Framed Question)

A framed question is one that builds on an assumption con-trary to what you assume the prospect believes. It is an extremely important interview tool because it gets you corrected, and get-ting you corrected not only gives you the right information but also encourages the dialogue with your prospect.

We have already noticed that when we ask people directly whether they are responsible for making decisions in a given area, they are likely to inflate their importance—at least dur-ing the first face-to-face meeting. People may not always be willing to give us the precise information we want, but we may rest assured that they will usually be willing to correct us and thus demonstrate their expertise.

During the sales interview, you should be ready to use a question that uses this principle to uncover information. This kind of question is *designed* to get you contradicted.

I realize the idea of posing a question that's meant to encourage the other person to contradict you sounds a little strange at first. But it does work, because human beings love to be right! So when you ask this kind of question, you're going to let the other person "right" you—and when he or she does so, mark my words, you'll get a whole long story about what's really going on in the organization.

Here's how it works. At a certain point, you're going to incorporate a specific assumption within the question or question sequence—an assumption that points in the opposite direction from the answer you "expect."

Framing can be adapted to virtually any type of information gap you need to fill. You can use this approach, for example, when you want to learn which, if any, of your competitors, your prospect is talking to. Here's what it might sound like.

> *You:* So, are you working with Plattsburgh Services to get a proposal together for this project?
>
> *Prospect:* Plattsburgh? No, no, they're way too small for a job like this. We're only talking to the bigger firms: yourself, Megacorp, ABC Development, and Business to Business. We had had some problems with the initial pricing Business to Business was talking about for this project, but our CEO used them exclusively at his last company, and he thinks very highly of their technical support team. So we had to get them in there.

Did you notice that the prospect, after correcting us, offered a little story that gave us some essential background information? My experience is that you'll be *much* more likely to get this kind of information if you ask a framed question than if you ask a question like "Who else are you talking to?"

Framed questions are designed to "harness" the other person's natural inclination to inflate his own importance, to be right, and to correct us. I recommend these questions for situations where you are having a little difficulty getting the other person to open up at the beginning of the meeting.

Again, how do you construct a framed question? Simply build in the assumption that you think the person is likely to correct, and then ask the question with the opposite assumption. Look at it again:

Question 68: I've spoken to your counterparts in other industries and they've got a preference for blue widgets. Have you found that to be the case?

The trick is to ask this when you already strongly suspect or have a good reason to believe that the person believes in yellow widgets. You see how it works? By "framing" the question so that it leads in the opposite direction of what you suspect the truth to be, you can encourage the other person to make a contribution to the conversation by correcting you: "No, we've always done business with the yellow widgets here. The reason we chose yellow widgets was . . ."

Obviously, you won't want to build in idiotic assumptions to your framed questions. ("Other people in your industry have told me that they are hoping for a nuclear apocalypse; is that what you'd like to see?")

You can use framed questions to develop essential information, and also get the person to contribute something meaningful to the conversation. It's a great way to build up momentum as the interviewing process moves forward.

Look at another example:

Question 69: A lot of the people I've spoken to in the shipping industry have told me that they feel that prospects for expanding in the European market are very limited. What's your take on that?

Obviously, you ask this when you are fairly confident the person's response is going to be something like the following:

"No! To the contrary, we feel that there is a lot of opportunity in Europe. Here's why . . ."

You've got a story to write down in your notes!

Frame a question and let the other person correct you. Remember: It is only by letting the other person "right" you that you can be absolutely *sure* you are on the right track.

Question 70: You don't mind if I take notes, do you?

Asking this question at an early point in the meeting, of course, is a perfectly acceptable way to set the tone. You may also choose to simply remove your yellow legal pad, pull out a pen, and begin writing down every word or key concept the other person shares with you.

I include the question here because many salespeople I train are skittish about taking notes without "permission." I'm not big on asking for "permission," but I suppose that if you are dealing with someone who is sensitive about revealing competitive information, or routinely handles materials that have legal or regulatory implications, it would probably be a good idea to confirm that the person has no problem with you taking notes.

In any event, you should make a point of recording, by hand, all the key points from the discussion. Doing so sends an impossible-to-ignore message: *I am listening to you.* Writing key points down during a meeting encourages your contact to open up, makes the conversation flow more smoothly, and it also establishes your credentials as someone who is willing to make a significant effort to get the right information down in black and white.

The Hidden Advantage

I think there is also a "hidden" advantage to taking down notes as I've described. The act of taking notes serves as a check for salespeople who are more inclined to talk than to listen. We have established that our goal is to make sure that the prospect does 80 percent of the talking. If we make a commitment to carry out the physical act of taking notes, it is much easier for us to turn that goal into a reality.

Finally, you may find that when your turn to speak does come around, the yellow legal pad is a uniquely effective sales tool. You can take the same pad you have been using to record your contact's insights and ideas and responses, fold it over, expose a clean page, and then explain your own points using the pad to deliver an impromptu visual display.

This notepad strategy is how we have sold the vast majority of our sales training programs at my company. It is a face-to-face, low-tech approach that I highly recommend. If you are careful to use the tool first as an information-gathering device, you will find that the transition to low-tech display unit can be a pretty seamless one and also one that effectively secures the attention of your contact. I cannot count the number of times I have finished taking notes for the bulk of the meeting then moved into the final phase of discussion by saying, "Let me show you what I'm thinking . . ." and developing a diagram on the spot that will help the prospect visualize what it is I am talking about.

Too many salespeople think that taking notes with a pen

and a piece of paper is "old school" selling. In fact, it is "new school" discipline for a salesperson whose goal is to get the other person to open up on a person-to-person level and also to prepare the way for forward movement in the sales cycle.

Question 71: Who did you work with last time?

It is amazing to me how many people come away from first appointments having no idea whether or not the prospect ever bought from someone else, or whether he is currently working with someone else. This is among the most fundamental issues in the world of sales, and if you walk away from the meeting without having determined it, you should be prepared to defend yourself in a lawsuit: for professional malpractice of a salesperson!

No matter what you are speaking to somebody about—a computer system, a shipping operation, a training program, an office coffee service, a health care plan for their employees—it is in your best interest to find out who this person has worked with in the past, if anyone. Sometimes people will tell me that they do not ask this question because they are afraid of abusing the prospect's confidentiality, or because they feel they do not know the person well enough to ask this question. This is nonsense. You must at least ask the question, and be prepared to see what kind of answer you get. Otherwise, you simply will not know where you stand! No working person with whom you should expect to do business will resent being asked this question, and if they do resent this question, you are perfectly justified in asking why they would not want to share the information with you.

Question 72: Why them?

An extremely important follow-through question. Simply getting the answer, "We work with ABC Company," *is not enough*. You must ask "Why them?" or some variation, in order to spark a dialogue and encourage the other person to open up to us. If you don't do that, two things will happen. Either the person will give us the information that you are after, or he or she will not give you this information, either because the contact does not know, or because there is a reason that he or she does not want you to know.

The point to remember, however, is that you simply cannot expect to move forward in a business relationship if the person will not share this kind of information with you. Remember, you are trying to get the other person to invest as much time, energy, information, and attention in the sales process as you are. You cannot expect to do that if you do not find out what led to the decision to work with a previous company.

If the person knows that their company is working with a competing vendor, if the person is aware of the existence of a current vendor, but cannot give you any insight whatsoever into the reasons for that vendor's selection, then you are talking to the wrong person and need to find a way to escalate the sale.

Question 73: Did you ever think about working with us?

This is another question that many salespeople are hesitant about asking. The only reason I can think that you would not want to ask it is that you *already know* that the person used to work with you in the past, and had a bad experience with you. If that is not the situation, and it usually is not, then there really is no reason on earth not to ask whether the person actually considered working with you before.

If he or she did think about working with you in the past, wouldn't you want to know what put you on the short list? Wouldn't you want to know why the person ended up going with someone else? Wouldn't you want to know how far in the selection process you got?

Of course, you should follow up this question with a relevant "how" or "why" question.

If you work for a company whose name is a household word—for instance, IBM, or GM, or Microsoft—it is perfectly appropriate to ask the person why he or she did not at least think about working with you in the past on a project. You do not want to phrase this question in a way that sounds arrogant or condescending, but you do want to follow through effectively, and find out what was guiding the person's selection of vendors, an area where you know you can add value, and know you have high visibility.

Question 74: How did you decide to handle challenge X the last time it came up with your vendor?

You are trying to get insights into the organization's decision-making process.

This question should be asked *after* the person tells you a story about something that went wrong in a previous vendor relationship. Your goal is to figure out how the organization responded, and what role your contact played in addressing the problem.

Question 75: Just to get a ballpark figure, what kind of budget are you working with?

When I suggest to salespeople that they pose this question during the first meeting, and preferably during the early portion of that meeting, they stare at me in horror. Among their responses:

- "I haven't even developed a rapport with the prospect yet."
- "The prospect doesn't know anything about us yet!"
- "I haven't had a chance to probe yet!"
- "I haven't determined what the person's needs are yet!"
- "I haven't determined what the person's 'pain' is yet!"

The prevailing thinking among so many salespeople today is that you cannot possibly discuss price in the most general or vague terms, without having engaged in some elaborate ritual. This ritual supposedly includes the determining of all the benchmarks and the criteria for success, as well as the "pain" or "need" that is keeping a person up at night, so you can craft a "value statement" that reflects the "cost" of doing business with your competition.

Nonsense.

The plain fact of the matter is that you have every right to ask, at least in general terms, whether or not this person has a budget that could result in the two of you working together. If this person does not know where or how big that budget is, or has a budget that is too small, you are in trouble. And you should know about that trouble early on, sooner rather than later.

If the person is not willing to tell you what the budget is, you are perfectly within your rights to ask or to say something like the following:

Question 76: Gee, I'm surprised to hear you say that. Usually people are very happy to tell me what kind of budget to work with, at least in general numbers so we can talk about a price range. Why wouldn't we want to talk about that?

Understand, please, that what I am suggesting that you do here is raise the *general* issue of price. We are not talking about engaging in a full-scale negotiation during the first meeting. That's impossible, anyway. It is not impossible, though, to determine whether or not the person with whom we are working is thinking in *roughly* the same terms that we are when it comes to dollar figures—within 25 percent, let's say, of the final figure.

We had a very successful salesperson once whose strategy on this front was much more aggressive than mine. After about 15 or 20 minutes of the first meeting, he would say, "Typically, what we charge for our training is X dollars, how does that sound?" He would then stop talking and see what happened.

Believe me when I tell you that all sorts of interesting things happened after he made this statement! If this person keeled over as if they were about to suffer a heart attack, he knew it probably did not make a lot of sense to continue having discussions with this person. And he wouldn't schedule a second meeting.

Wouldn't you want to know, upfront, that there is going to be a 75 percent discrepancy between what you think you are going to charge and what the prospect thinks you are going to charge? Why wouldn't you want to know about that during the first meeting?

Question 77: What is your timeline?

Just as essential as getting a ballpark sense of the budget's importance is the task of determining a ballpark sense of *when* the person wants something to happen. If you don't have this kind of information, or if the person is unwilling or unable to share it with you, *that person is statistically unlikely to become your customer.*

You could also phrase the question like this:

Question 78: If you and I were to decide to work together, what would the calendar for that look like?

Again, you do not have to go through a huge mating dance in order to have the "right" to ask this question. *You must determine for yourself whether this person is worth coming back to meet with again.*

The only way to do that is to figure out whether or not the timeline and the money makes sense, at least in general terms. If you do not know whether the timeline matches up with your average selling cycle, you should.

YOUR QUESTIONING STRATEGY

The longer your discussions with any given contact go *beyond* your average selling cycle, the less likely you are to close the sale.

That doesn't mean you never close a deal that takes twelve weeks, if your cycle is eight weeks. But the sales that go beyond eight weeks are an anomaly. We typically invest more time and effort beyond our selling cycle than the payoff justifies. Choose where you invest your time. It's precious.

Why is the comparison to the average selling cycle so important? Because, whether we care to acknowledge it or not, our success in sales has a certain mathematical pattern that plays out on the calendar. In the sales training industry, we know that a deal will go from our first meeting to receive a signed contract in an average time period of between six and eight weeks. That is extremely important for us to know from a strategic point of view. Why? Because it is a hard and unavoidable statistical fact, born out by our own direct experience, that the longer a sale goes beyond that time period, the less likely it is to close.

While we're on the subject, you should ask the *prospect* . . .

Question 79: What is your average sales cycle?

A fair number of the people you ask this question will not be familiar with the term "sales cycle" so you may have to explain to them that what you are talking about is the amount of time it takes them to move from initial contact or first discussion, to a decision to purchase. You can expect to get an answer that begins with the words "It depends . . ." when you ask this question, but you should also be prepared to press, ever so tactfully, for some kind of meaningful explanation of where the upper and lower boundaries lie.

I have worked with companies whose sales cycle was 20 minutes (their upper-end duration of a telesales appeal). I have also worked with companies whose sales cycle was upward of two years. The answer you receive will tell you a great deal about the culture of the organization, and the processes it must implement to attract customers, keep them happy, and begin the process all over again.

If you do not have a good sense of how long it takes a given company to turn a prospect into a customer, you should not expect to be treated as a business ally in any meaningful sense of the word. Make a point of getting some kind of response to this question, whether or not the answer directly relates to your product or service. It is important strategic information.

Question 80: Do you personally do a lot of (long-distance calling)? (Assuming that you are selling telecommunications.)

This is a question designed to help you identify how much or how little contact your prospect will have with your product or service. It's important to determine how much actual exposure your prospect will have to what you deliver.

Question 81: What kinds of concerns do you personally have about (the team's performance)?

This is another excellent question to encourage somebody to share a story with you, but you have to be sure to focus it correctly. The key is to focus in on some area where you know you can have value, preferably value that some other competitor has not got a great record of delivering. So, for instance:

Question 82: What kind of concerns do you have about hitting your sales quota this year?

Or . . .

Question 83: What kind of concerns do you have about managing your communications with your sales force during the time that the merger is underway?

Or . . .

Question 84: What kind of concerns do you have about reaching out to the Eastern European market?

You will find this kind of question to be most effective when you ask your "concern" a question about something that the contact has already expressed some misgivings or uncertainty about. Always show great concern for whatever the prospect is concerned about!

Your Questioning Strategy

Find out what they are concerned about, and then be more concerned about it than they are!

We can't just ask "What keeps you up at night?" although some people do open the meeting that way. It's far better to get the other person to tell you a story, then ask specifically what he or she is concerned about or anxious about with regard to that story.

Exploring the Contact's Key Concerns

If we say to the person, "What is it you are trying to get accomplished this year?" and then hear the executive or the decision-maker take as a major goal the switch over to a new computer system, then we are perfectly within our rights to ask: *What kind of concerns specifically do you have about that transition?*

At that point, we are asking the kind of question that people within the contact company very rarely ask, namely, "What could go wrong?"

That is the kind of question that an executive or senior decision-maker *has* to ask himself or herself, but it is comparatively rare that he runs into people who will volunteer to ask that kind of question. You know why—if you ask that question in your own work environment, you are very likely to find yourself "delegated" with the responsibility of resolving the problem you have just unearthed! But as a salesperson, our goal is to emerge as "virtual employees"—that is to say, people who step up and act not only like employees, but as advocates for the executive's point of view and areas of concern. So when we ask, specifically, what kinds of concerns do you have about how that transition might work, it is a more informed question than simply asking, "What keeps you up at night?" The reason is that we have identified something specific in the person's world that he or she is trying to make happen. We are presenting ourselves as someone who will help evaluate potential problems and challenges, and who will be *more* concerned than even the decision-maker is about the problems that may arise in implementing our contact's ideas.

This strategy works particularly well when you really are dealing with someone who has senior decision-making authority, and who has a clear mandate to implement your product or service. If you ask a technical type or an engineer to show you all the possible things that could go wrong with a given initiative, you may well get a long lecture back that details the thousand possible data points that could be flawed, and must be double-checked by means of doing spreadsheets, conducting sixteen different regression analyses. That is why I stay away from this kind of question when I am dealing with engineers, programmers, and other technical people. But if I am talking to somebody whose time is short, whose resources are scarce, and whose authority is obvious—in other words, if I am talking to someone with executive authority whose to-do list is long and whose ambitions are significant—I will be more than willing to ask a follow-up question that focuses on a specific area of concern in an area that this *executive* has raised. I will then show the same level of concern, or even more concern, than that person has shown.

Later in the sales process, when it comes time to close the sale, I will make a point of returning to the concerns and issues that executive raised, and I will be more concerned about it than my contact is, or at least try to be. But here is the key to making that kind of close work: *I have to know, in the other person's words, what really does concern him or her.* And as we have seen, it takes a little effort to identify the areas of importance and then uncover all the possible areas of uncertainty or concern within the subject area our contact has already raised. If we try to paste on concerns or worries that do not really belong to this person, but belong to somebody else we spoke to two weeks ago, we will not gather much meaningful information, and we simply will not have a platform from which to express our own concerns at the end of the sales process.

Question 85: What are the biggest challenges you personally are facing with this project?

This is a variation on the earlier question about what concerns the other person, but note the subtle shift in emphasis. Here we are asking about the personal challenges that our contact is facing as an individual. This is another great opportunity to unearth stories from the person's background or experience, stories that may shed insight on how he or she evaluates the project, or indeed how he or she looks at the world. It is quite possible, of course, that you may get a one- or two-word answer to a question like this. Do not be afraid to encourage the other person to expand on his or her answer by asking . . .

Question 86: Why is that the biggest challenge?

If you ask somebody, "What is your biggest challenge in securing and getting this new sales office up and running?" it is quite possible that the person will think carefully for a moment, look you in the eye, and say "Personnel."

What does that kind of an answer mean? It means the person you're talking to typically does not offer much information to a broad initial question, but that does not necessarily mean you have hit a dead end. Your job as a salesperson is to pursue the lead until you have exhausted all the possible avenues for gathering information. So at this point you should ask, "Okay—what specifically about personnel makes that the most important challenge?"

To get someone to expand on a brief response, you could also structure the question this way:

Question 87: A lot of your counterparts at organizations in this industry have told me that their biggest personnel challenge when it comes to salespeople is developing the right incentive program. Is that your experience as well?

Nine times out of ten, this will generate some kind of interesting response. If the person still gives you a short or noncommittal answer, it is very likely that you have more rapport-building work to do, or that you are meeting with someone who will not become a meaningful business ally.

Question 88: Who is your ideal customer?

This is the kind of question that can flummox administrative or technical types, but that will instantly elicit a clear, powerful, and impossible-to-misunderstand response from senior executives and people charged with sales and marketing responsibilities. By posing it, you can identify who's who, and also get a clear sense of the market that the company is trying to reach. A good follow-up question is . . .

Question 89: What kinds of new customers are you trying to attract?

Another question the CEO or VP of marketing will be able to rhapsodize on at length. Encourage this—and take notes!

If you find that the person with whom you are speaking is uncertain about how to answer the question, there is a very good chance that he or she lacks significant decision-making authority, and it may be time to try to move on to someone else.

Question 90: How would you describe your ideal customer?

An interesting variation. If you do not feel comfortable asking your contact to identify what specific marketing efforts are underway, you can always use this question.

Question 91: Who is your most important prospect right now?

The unspoken question, of course, has to do with the difference between a prospect and a customer. You should be willing to discuss this, as well.

This is a query that is most likely to be of direct interest to people with responsibility for attracting and retaining customers. It is also a good question to pose to any senior decision-maker and will give you important insights on how the company is positioning itself in the market.

Question 92: What is your most important target market?

A good question to ask if you are trying to get a sense of the company's marketing and sales priorities. Even if your product or service has nothing to do with sales and marketing, it is a good idea to know what the firm identifies as its most important market. If the person you are talking to does not know, the odds are good that he or she does not have much in the way of decision-making authority.

Question 93: What are you trying to do to reach that market?

Again, most people with formal or informal decision-making authority will be able to answer this question without any difficulty. If your contact hesitates or offers a selection of bland platitudes about "ongoing promotions," you are well advised to try to find some way to work your way up to try to meet with someone else in the organization.

Question 94: Who are your most important suppliers/vendors?

It is important, as well, to get a fix on the key vendor and supplier relationships that make the company's mission possible. Every company has a list of allies, vendors, and suppliers. If you plan to establish yourself as a meaningful long-term partner or resource, it is definitely in your interest to determine who those vendors and partners are. Find out about manufacturers, consultants, and organizations with whom the target firm has established critical marketing alliances.

Question 95: How long have you been with the company?

This is a question that can reveal much more than you might think. If it is not used as part of the "pleasantry" phase, it should be worked into the body of the meeting at some point.

This question helps you tell the difference between someone who has a good deal of experience in a given career field, and someone who has a lot of experience with the organization. These are two very different things. It is quite possible to hook up with a decision-maker who looks and sounds as though he or she has been "on the inside" for many years, when in fact the person is still getting acclimated to the culture of the organization you are trying to sell to.

Take a few moments to explore not just how the person has gotten the job, but also what level of experience he or she has within the company. Even someone with superb financials "on paper" who has no real idea how to make things happen within the organization's informal chain of command will probably not be helpful to you in moving the sale forward.

Question 96: How do you like the job?

Not, as you might imagine, an "icebreaker" question. You should withhold this until you have the chance to connect with the prospect as a person, and are well into the "business" portion of the meeting. It is a great question for unearthing stories that reveal this person's take on his work, the target company, and the industry as a whole.

A slightly less direct variation is the following:

Question 97: What is it like to work here?

Basically, you're asking about the corporate culture. You may be surprised at how dramatically the answers you receive about a company's culture will vary, depending on whom you ask.

This can be asked as a follow-up to Question 96.

Question 98: How many people work in this department/division/branch?

If you have a good sense of how many people work in a given operation, you will begin to get a sense of how big an operation you are dealing with.

If you feel it is appropriate to do so, you should continue along the following lines:

Question 99: How many of these people report to you?

Or . . .

Question 100: How many of these people work with you?

Warning: This is important information, but we no longer live in a world in which we can judge a person's importance by the number of people who salute him or her in the morning.

All the same, we should probably have some sense of the person's network, formal or informal, and the number of people who report to or work with him or her. Particularly if your practical solution affects the team numbers who operate under this individual, you will want to know approximately . how many people you are dealing with.

Of course, it is true that there may be many important people within the organization to whom no one reports, at least technically. (A former CEO who serves as an informal "adviser," for instance.)

In the right settings, Questions 99 and/or 100 will come off as flattering, and will tell you a great deal about the person and the organization.

Question 101: How many other locations do you have?

The number of salespeople who come back from their first meeting without any understanding of whether they are dealing with a single outlet or a branch of a larger company is really astonishing to me.

This is one of those questions that affects the daily life of every one of your prospects, so you really should not skip it. Try to get some sense of the organization's network, where the corporate headquarters is, and how procurement/purchasing decisions in your area have been handled in the past. Even if all the purchasing is centralized, and you know you will be dealing with the central location, and even if you know for certain that all the purchasing decisions can be handled by the person with whom you are speaking, it is important to get a basic understanding of who operates where.

Question 102: Can I tell you a little bit about why I chose to work with this company?

This is an excellent question you can use when you want to tell a story of your own. (Before you use it, be sure you are not violating the interviewer's 80/20 rule!)

You should use this question to share a story that reinforces a key point about your decision to work with your firm, a point that is directly relevant to this person's situation or challenge. The story you share should connect, in other works, with a core value that relates directly to your prospect's challenge. For instance, if you decided to join the company because you were drawn to its reputation for high quality and intolerance for error, this would be a good point to share with a prospect who has no tolerance for mistakes and is in search of a perfect quality record.

It is a good idea, as we have seen, to have a number of relevant stories in the hopper. Each of these should be preceded by an appropriate question. For instance:

Question 103: Can I tell you a little bit about why XYZ Company decided to work with us?

A classic transition question. This can lead, seamlessly, to a story that you select that is directly relevant to a concern or issue faced by the prospect.

You should be ready to discuss, at any moment, the stories of between six and twelve actual companies who have worked with your firm. It is important to be able to discuss the decisions that went into these purchase choices in some detail, and to be able to supply references, if possible. If you are uncertain about the details, write them down and memorize them!

Question 104: Who would you say is your most important competitor?

The prospect's assessment of who the company should regard as its chief competition will tell you a great deal about the individual and the market.

It is an interesting fact of sales life that the perceptions of who the competition is will sometimes change radically, depending on whom you ask in the organization. So, as you move through the company, be ready to restate this question (tactfully, if the meeting includes your original prospect). Try to get as many viewpoints as possible. Write them all down.

Question 105: Where do you think the economy is going?

This is a broad-based question that will give your prospect a chance to hold forth on what the future holds for the country as a whole. A fair percentage of the people with whom you will be meeting will welcome the chance to take on the role of the "expert," and this question offers them a perfect opportunity to do so. Take plenty of notes.

As your contact is sharing insights, it is quite likely that he or she will also share stories that illustrate his or her outlook, goals, position in the company, and level of experience. Write all this down, too.

Question 106: Where do you think this industry is going?

This is a more focused, and perhaps more pertinent, variation on Question 105. It carries all the potential benefits of that question, with the additional advantage that it will help you determine the contact strategy for dealing with recent industry trends.

If you have asked one of these questions, you probably should not ask the other in quick succession. Space things out, and follow through intelligently with "how" and "why" questions that build on the responses you hear from your contact.

Question 107: Does your company have any plans to expand?

A good question to ask when you know that times are good in the industry in which your prospect is operating. Obviously, if you are certain the industry in question is going through a major shakeout, you should avoid this question, and perhaps consider asking . . .

Question 108: How is your company dealing with the challenges in this industry?

CEOs, presidents, and other chief executives tend to answer this with frankness and surprising measures of optimism. Mid-level functionaries, on the other hand, are likely to think first and foremost about their own departments, companies, or job positions—and to conceal those concerns imperfectly.

The body language of the person to whom you pose this question will also be quite revealing. If you are in discussions with someone who tenses up and starts stammering, or shows other signs of stress and indecision when you raise this question, it is a good bet that he or she is not in a position to serve as a major advocate for pushing your ideas through to other people in the company at a time when the organization faces serious economic obstacles.

If you are prospecting to companies that are in a market that faces significant industry challenges, you should make a special effort to identify and speak with players in that organization who are willing to look at new initiatives and creative approaches. Remember, there is really not much point in spending a good deal of your time with someone who will not help you move forward in the sales process.

Question 109: How do you think (problem *X*/challenge *X*) happened?

A follow-up for use when a prospect shares the details of a recent company trauma. Pose it carefully and tactfully.

Try finding what lessons a person or the organization has learned from a major setback; this may be important information when it comes time to draft your proposal or outline, where you will want to focus on the prospect's personal assessment of a major trial or challenge.

Always remember that your goal is to get the person to tell you stories about his or her world, so you can match up your organization's own best stories with those events and the lessons that have been learned from them.

Question 110: How did you end up with the system you're using now?

Often, salespeople will be called in to help adapt, update, or replace an existing way of doing things with which no one in the target organization is really happy. When we face this sort of situation, it is tempting to focus only on the logistical questions of how we can develop a new system that will work better, or which constituencies we will be able to keep happy by doing so. It is just as important, and perhaps even more so, however, to ask what led to the development and implementation of the old way of doing things. If you do not know that, it is very possible that you will repeat an earlier mistake, and lose the account.

Question 111: How did this (system) get (installed/tested/analyzed)?

For certain types of decision-makers, this seemingly innocuous question, and intelligent variations on it, represents a great opportunity for major bonding with a salesperson.

It will happen from time to time that you find yourself face-to-face with a senior decision-maker who clearly has the authority to make happen what you want to make happen, and who also has what might best be described as a technical or analytic mindset. If you find yourself in such a situation, this is the sort of question you will want to ask.

Some people live to explain and analyze the "how" of technical issues. They love to focus on the potential problems of implementation, of all the careful trial runs necessary to make sure implementation will be a success, and all of the "looking around corners" they personally undertook in a given initiative. It is a mistake to assume that people who focus on the technical details in this way are always micromanagers who "cannot see the big picture." Quite a fair number of high-powered executives work from this mindset. Never, ever attempt to speed past the details with such people.

Keep an eye out for signs, direct or indirect, of disasters he or she helped to avert, problems he or she helped to keep from happening in the first place, and the dire outcome of failing to listen to his or her advice. These are the kinds of stories that such a decision-maker tends to focus on. With such people, it is very important to allow them to hold forth on the "how" of a current system or procedure, and to get all the necessary insights about the ways in which they would avoid a problem if it were being done again. The question I have provided can be adapted in any number of ways, but what is most important is that you allow the person to share his or her main priorities in analyzing, troubleshooting, and re-evaluating all the possible data points that could, if unexamined, lead to disaster.

A final note of warning is in order when dealing for sales that require the approval of such decision-makers. These are people who live to find fault, identify unanticipated problems, and shoot down projects. A meeting is not a success, at least for some of these folks, until they have found something to reject as unworkable. Spotting flaws is their meat and drink!

It is, therefore, in your interest to identify, not one, but three or four potential ways of working together, thereby allowing you to focus the discussion on which of the measures you eventually propose is the soundest—and allowing your contact the duty (and pleasure) of spotting flaws in the other possibilities you suggest.

Question 112: How do you see (X) problem?

This is another good question to share with those who have a deeply analytical mindset. Asking an analytical decision-maker to share his or her analysis of a problem will work wonders in building bridges.

If you have hooked up, however, not with an analytical executive, but rather with a hard-charging, forceful, take-charge executive, it is quite possible that he or she will respond to this question by changing the subject to another problem that is more important . . . or by demanding that you address the problem you have raised. Be prepared for both possibilities.

Question 113: Have you ever worked with an outsider on a project like this before?

Sales training. Advertising. Project design. Customer service/call center work. Distribution. Public relations.

These days, companies outsource just about anything and everything, in order to stay focused on what they themselves do the best. The idea is to identify those tasks that are not supported by the company's own critical strengths. Once you have identified the tasks that aren't playing to your own strengths, you can find someone else to do them.

All very well in theory. But, if this is the very first time that someone has been brought in from the outside to train new employees, you will want to know what the training procedures were over the past fifteen or so years. If this is the first time that the company has ever brought somebody in from the outside to handle customer calls, you will want to know the details about that, too.

If you are looking at a situation where outsiders *have* been brought in before, find out who was chosen or considered last time, what got them on the short list, and how the final decision was made.

Question 114: How long have you been trying to . . . ?

If someone tells you that he is pursuing a strategic goal, one that is important both to his future and the future of the company, that goal came from somewhere, and it arose at a certain point in time. Is this something the person adopted as his or her primary aim last night? Two weeks ago? A month ago? A year ago?

Question 115: Just out of curiosity, what makes this a top priority for you personally?

What specifically caused the person to adopt this goal in the first place? Was it because the CEO took on the job of pounding it into everyone's head? Because the newest hot shot recruited to the team insisted it was the best way to go? Is this dream your prospect's personal creation? Who will get credit for the initiative if it succeeds? Who will be held accountable for failure?

Major goals and initiatives do not emerge from a vacuum. Do your best to determine when they were born and to whom, and what their implications are to your prospect and to others in the organization.

Question 116: What would you think is the most important project/initiative you are working on right now?

An extremely important question whose answers can be arrived at indirectly by means of any number of the questions posed in this book. However, if you reach the halfway point of your first meeting with a prospect, and you realize that you do not yet have any idea what the most important initiative in your prospect's world is, you are certainly well advised to pose this question.

The question carries with it a number of important follow-up questioning opportunities, including:

Question 117: How does this initiative affect your salespeople and your marketing efforts?

There are a very few major undertakings that do not ultimately connect with an organization's marketing and sales professionals. By posing this question, you may be able to shine some light on an issue that directly relates to the company's marketing and sales efforts, which are, of course, essential to its success and survival.

Question 118: How does this initiative affect your logistics and operations team?

Depending on the size of the organization, you may want to scale this question so that it refers to the administrative support staff, the shipping or warehousing team, or the frontline customer service staff. The point is that whatever initiative you undercover as being the most important for the team, it will inevitably have an impact on the people whose job it is to actually carry out the vision that will deliver products and services and keep customers happy.

Question 119: How does this initiative affect your recruiting or retention efforts?

In midsize or smaller companies, this may not be a particularly important concern. In large organizations, however, the retention of human capital is likely to be a key strategic goal, and any new initiative that your prospect is pursuing may well carry implications in this area. Sometimes key constituencies are demoralized by change in focus; sometimes resources designed to help retain or attract key people have to be pointed in a new direction. Especially if you are dealing with a senior decision-maker, you will find that exploring these avenues helps you to establish trust and rapport with your contact. These are precisely the kinds of questions that keep CEOs and other key decision-makers up at night!

Question 120: How does your company sell its products or services?

Sometimes salespeople astonish me. I have had conversations during training programs with people who have assured me that their "number 1 prospect" is such-and-such a company, and who assured me in the same breath that they are "in control of the deal" and that they know everything of consequence about the company in question.

When I ask the salesperson how his or her company attracts customers in the first place, I hear a long silence, followed by a queasy response: "Promotion." Or: "Advertising, I think." Or: "I am pretty sure they have a national sales staff, but they may work through distributors, I am not quite sure."

If you do not know *exactly* how your prospect company sells its products or service, you are not in a good position to sell your product or service to that company! Get all the details. Is there a network of field reps? Inside salespeople? Does the company sell through distributors? Do those distributors have an incentive program of any kind? Is there a nationwide direct-mail campaign? A series of Internet pop-up ads? An opt-in e-mail list? A combination of all of these elements?

You know and I know that there is no single, simple answer to this question. But that is what makes it so very important. We have to identify exactly what marketing and sales mix our prospect company has settled on, at least in the short term, so we can put ourselves in the position of the senior decision-makers, who rely on those marketing and sales methods to deliver revenue and keep the company afloat. If we have no idea what these techniques for winning customers are, we should not expect the company's business to go to someone who isn't willing to find out this critical business information.

Question 121: How important are repeat sales to your company?

You will want to apply this question selectively, adapting it to situations where you are aware that there is some kind of repeat-business imperative within the organization. To be sure, this applies to most companies, but there are exceptions. Once you identify how important a customer's decision to return to the company again really is, you will want to continue with effective follow-up questions that identify the specific retention and reward programs that have been set up to maintain and extend relationships to customers.

It is a fact of business life, at least in most industries, that it costs far less to retain a customer than it does to track down a new one. You should use some variation of this question to get a sense of the specific issues your prospect faces in keeping customers happy and keeping them coming back for more.

Question 122: What are you doing to hold on to your best customers?

An obvious follow-up to Question 121. Be prepared to offer stories about how other companies who worked with you were able to develop effective strategies for retaining customers or reducing overall attrition.

Question 123: How are you going to use this?

It is common for salespeople to receive a request for a certain product, component, or installation—without having any idea of what larger purpose the purchase will serve. The same thing applies, though less frequently, to purchases of services.

With my company, people purchase training for a variety of reasons. These include:

- To increase retention
- To improve performance in a specific area
- To motivate the team to embrace a new product
- To prove to a superior that they are taking action in a certain area
- To get one sales team to start performing as another one does
- To use up money in their budget that will evaporate if they don't use it by a certain point in time
- Because they don't know what else to do with staff people they've just inherited

Which is it?

If you want to have an ongoing relationship with someone, it is in your best interest to determine how specifically what you are selling will be used.

Question 124: What are you doing right now to improve your profile in the marketplace?

A question you should consider asking—tactfully, of course—if the company has recently faced public relations problems or market setbacks, and if you are in a position to help address its challenges on either front.

Question 125: Can I tell you what some of your counterparts in the organizations that we have been working with are concerned about in this area?

This is a transitional question designed to help you introduce a relevant success story. Obviously, you will want to avoid sharing anything that is even close to being confidential business information, but there is a great deal more you can do to share information and insights, especially by passing along stories from companies that do not directly compete with one another.

You really are an expert. You really do have a right to pass along such information, and to analyze it for your prospect. This is one of the exciting things about working in sales. After you have been with it for only a very limited amount of time—say six or eight weeks—you realize you and your organization really do have a wealth of direct, practical experience that some of your prospects will definitely benefit from hearing. Do not be afraid to volunteer relevant advice and success stories that have come about as a result of working with other companies. Too often, salespeople seem to be apologizing for even stepping into the prospect's office when they should, by rights, be charging consulting fees!

You are an expert in what you do. If you were not, you would not be making a living this way. You know your industry, and you know your product or service, and the odds are that you know enough relevant situations to this one to be able to add value to the person's operation. Think of yourself as less of a convincer and as more of a specialist, someone with valuable experience that can be brought to bear in any number of different professional settings.

Intelligent variations on this question include:

Question 126: Can I tell you how some of my clients in the (*X*) industry dealt with this problem?

Or . . .

Question 127: Can I share with you how we handled this when we faced a similar situation with (ABC Company)? *Or* Can I give you the highlights of a case study we did that was very similar to this?

Or . . .

Question 128: Can I tell you about something that happened to me that may be helpful?

Or . . .

Question 129: Can I tell you what my boss did about this when he faced the same situation?

All of these are excellent transitional questions. Tailor them to match the story you are hoping to share.

YOUR QUESTIONING STRATEGY

When sharing a success story with a prospect . . .

- Paint a picture
- Emphasize the benefit
- Keep it brief
- Hit the essential points
- Ask for feedback

Question 130: Can I tell you why I ask that question?

Another excellent transitional question that positions you to share a relevant success story. I have gotten good results by following this question with phrases like the following:

- What I am getting is . . .
- Here is what I am hearing . . .
- If we are on the same page, and I think we are, what we are looking at is . . .

Following an explanatory phrase like this, I will explain the line of reasoning that has led me to this point, laying special emphasis on the kinds of problems that my company has been able to help other people in this person's situation resolve.

It is extremely important, though, to understand that you cannot rush this moment in the meeting—the moment where you start to share your own ideas about how you and the prospect may be able to work together. There's a paradox at work here: You can't rush the moment, but you do need to make sure it happens.

YOUR QUESTIONING STRATEGY

You cannot know ahead of time when it will make sense for you to make a first attempt to "shine a spotlight" on your company and its capabilities. Realize, however, that this is not to be confused with your initial "commercial" about you and your firm, which should only take approximately 30 seconds. In the ideal situation, you will start to share success stories only after you have the chance to take a fair amount of notes and your prospect has opened up about the business challenges he or she faces. Most importantly, you should listen to your "audience" and find out for yourself when it is ready for you to move on to this phase of the "show."

Question 131: What is on the horizon?

You can ask effective follow-ups to this question and focus on the company, the department, the team, or the individual. My personal preference is to ask it in an open-ended fashion, as above.

Simply by posing the question, and not qualifying exactly whom or what I am talking about, I get all kinds of interesting information in return. Sometimes, people will share their deepest personal hopes, dreams, and career aspirations; sometimes, they will go into an in-depth competitive analysis for me. This is a great question, one that encourages people to share truly meaningful insights. It is not, however, something you can use to open the meeting, because it depends on a certain amount of rapport and trust having been established.

In this chapter, I've given you what I hope is a good overview of "do-based" questions that will be helpful models for you to use during the main part of a meeting when you drop in on the prospect. But what if the prospect drops in on you, or calls you? Although many of the same principles will apply, there are some special question categories you should be ready to use during that kind of discussion. Let's examine those in the next chapter.

Chapter Five

Questions to Figure Out What Someone Who Contacts *You* Does

W hen a field sales representative calls a lead and sets a date and time for a first appointment, there is a certain predictable dynamic at work. A similar dynamic is at work when we meet that person face-to-face for the first time. But when the prospect calls you, walks into your store, or drops in unannounced at your office, there is a very different dynamic to understand.

In this chapter, you'll get a look at some of the questions you can use to identify what is really going on in the world of this kind of prospect.

Inbound Telesales Questions

Question 132: Just out of curiosity, what made you decide to call us?

This is an excellent all-purpose question for anyone whose business relies on face-to-face discussions with retail customers, but it can just as easily be applied to someone who wanders into a trade booth or sends your company an e-mail after visiting your Web site. The trick is to find out what has recently changed in this person's life: What he or she encountered, decided, or had to solve or change that resulted in the *decision* to contact you.

After all, he didn't contact you because he didn't have anything else to do! Something changed. Your job is to find out what that "something" is.

Effective variations include:

Question 133: Can I ask how you heard about us?

Or . . .

Question 134: Had you ever thought about working with us before?

Or . . .

Question 135: I'm just curious, what made you decide to get in touch with us about . . . ?

Or . . .

Question 136: I'm just curious, what made you decide to take action in this area?

Or . . .

Question 137: I'm just curious, what made you decide to get a quote for (replacing the windows in your home)?

If you don't ask some variation on this "What changed?" question very early on in the conversation, you will not gain any meaningful depth of information from your prospect.

YOUR QUESTIONING STRATEGY

The "What changed?" question category is particularly important for telesales representatives who handle inbound calls from prospects.

Something made the marketing message "click" with your prospect. The closer you come to identifying what that is, the more you will be likely to sell to this person.

Question 138: By the way, have you heard about our . . . ?

A classic "upselling" question to use at the end of a good telesales call. You've gone to all the trouble and effort of establishing a good relationship with this person. Why not mention an ancillary product or service and ask whether that might be a good match for the prospect's situation?

The words "by the way" are important to any upselling effort in a telesales environment, as they lower the pressure. Use them!

Retail Questions

Question 139: What made you decide to stop by today?

Finding out what made the person decide to visit your store is essential. During my training sessions with salespeople, I tell the following story, which illustrates the importance of these kinds of questions.

Two Retail Discussions

Some time ago, I wandered into a Brooks Brothers store to buy a pair of suspenders. That was ALL I wanted to buy. I made my way to the counter, and the salesman there stared at me blankly. I said, "Suspenders." He pointed and said, "Over there."

So I walked "over there," in the direction he had pointed. I picked out a single pair of suspenders. I paid for them. I left the store.

I then went to an electronics store. Once again, my aim was pretty simple: I wanted to buy a basic clock radio. Nothing else.

A pleasant-looking young salesperson in the store smiled at me as I approached and welcomed me to the store.

I tend to be very direct. True to form, I said "Clock radios."

Now, remember that this really was all I wanted to buy. And yet, at that point in the conversation, something startling happened. The salesperson said, "Just out of curiosity, what brought you into the store today?"

I have to admit—I wasn't ready for that question! She was actually interested in what had changed in my life enough to ask me what had brought me into the store. The question stopped me cold, but I answered it. I explained that I had just moved to the area, and that, since my place was mostly empty, I had no way of waking up in the morning. So I wanted to buy a clock radio.

She showed me the clock radios. I picked out a model. Then she asked me whether I wanted to look at a television set. Well, that certainly made sense. "Sure," I said. "Why don't you show me where those are and let me take a look at what you have."

There were other questions as well. Did I want to look at CD players? Microwave ovens? Cordless telephones?

An hour after having walked into a store intending only to buy a $20 clock radio, I left with $2,000 in merchandise.

Why?

Because one woman had the sense to ask me about what I had done that had caused me to *change my pattern* and walk into her store.

It should be obvious enough to you by now that, if you do any kind of retail selling work, you should start asking this question. Intelligent variations on this question include:

Question 140: Hi there, I'm Mike. Are you looking for something for your (husband)?

Suppose you own a men's store. How should you approach a woman walking purposefully through your tie section? Before you answer, stop and think for a moment about the number of times you yourself have stepped into a store and been asked, "Can I help you?"

If you're like most of us, you've been asked that question hundreds, maybe thousands of times. How often did you say, "Yes"? Hardly ever, I'd bet.

So: Why ask someone wandering through your store, "Can I help you?" Let's face it, the person is hardwired to respond, "No, I'm just looking."

This question offers a different approach: Be friendly. Introduce yourself.

Look closely, and you'll notice that this is (or at least can be) a framed question. The person is going to say, "No, no, I'm not looking for anything for him—my son's entering a private school this week, and he needs a tie for an orientation dinner he's going to."

We can then follow up with:

Question 141: Oh, okay—just out of curiosity, has your (son) got (anything to wear for formal dances)?

Do you see how it works? By allowing the prospect to correct you, you get a better picture of what's happening in his or her world, and you're in a better position to have a meaningful conversation about how you might be able to help.

Question 142: Do you see anything you can't absolutely live without?

I love this question—because it's a guaranteed conversation-starter in a retail setting. Look at it closely. The question is designed to make it easy for the other person to respond by saying "No, not really." That's important, because that's the answer people want to give already—it's the answer to the question they're used to being asked: "Can I help you?"

But look what happens when the person tells us, "No, not really." We're in a perfect position to move the conversation forward! Look at the follow-through question:

Question 143: I didn't think so. (Little pause.) Can I show you something?

Wow! We've connected with the other person, we've let them give us the initial negative response, the response they're conditioned to give, and we've begun an interaction. Most people say "Sure," when you ask them this question! That means you're in a great position to show off the most impressive or noteworthy thing in the store, find out what they think of it, and start getting a sense of what's driving the person's visit.

All of a sudden, you're in a conversation! This is a very effective question sequence for the retail environment. Try it.

"Do-Based" Questions for Managers Only

Okay, okay—in a pinch, nonmanagers can read this section, too. But managers are the only ones who will really be able to put it to good use.

The point for managers (and anyone else) to understand is that the "do-based" questions we have been examining don't just become part of somebody's routine overnight. They must be reinforced. And the only practical way of reinforcing them (other than taking a training session, or reading this book over and over again) is for managers to ask some questions of their own during sales meetings.

So—without further ado—here are the critical questions sales managers should learn to *ask their salespeople* during each and every sales meeting.

Here's my guarantee to you: If you make a habit of asking

these questions *during* each meeting then your salespeople will make a habit of finding out the answers—by means of the "do-based" questions I've been talking about in this book—*before* each meeting.

Questions to Ask Salespeople about Their Prospects

Question 144: When are you going back?

If they have no idea, it's not a real prospect. Period. Don't let them project income from the lead in question.

Question 145: What does the company do? *Or* Who are its customers?

So. They say they've met with these folks, but they don't know what the company sells or which companies they work with. Be skeptical. Be very, very skeptical.

Question 146: Who are you talking to?

The trouble signs here tend to come in two varieties. First, the "huge cast of characters" trouble sign: When you ask this question, people start talking about everyone in the target organization, from the receptionist to the senior widget engineer. Second, the "I'm still figuring that out" trouble sign: When you ask this question, the salesperson starts talking about connections and referrals but can't actually name anyone who's moving the sales cycle forward. If there is not a single clear ally who is willing to schedule time to talk with your salesperson, don't project income from the lead.

Question 147: Why that person?

In a perfect world, the answer is that the person either has made a decision like this in the past or can get the decision made for us now.

Question 148: How long has your contact been there?

If they don't know, then they don't know anything of consequence about the contact's ability to get things done within the target organization.

Question 149: What, specifically, is this company doing now in an area where we can add value?

There really are people out there who like to talk to salespeople, but who don't ever give them any meaningful information. Be sure your sales rep isn't investing weeks of time and effort with such a person. *Information and access are indicators of interest!*

Question 150: Why aren't they using us already?

It's a fair question, one to which your salesperson should have some kind of intelligent response.

Question 151: When was your first meeting?

Remember—the longer the discussion extends beyond your average sales cycle, the less likely the prospect is to buy.

Question 152: Did you call them or did they call you?

Basic information that a professional salesperson is unlikely to forget. If the salesperson "doesn't remember," there is a chance—but only a chance—that there is no real sales opportunity at all here, or perhaps no real contact! Ask to call the prospect yourself. If the salesperson turns white with fear, you may have bigger problems than a dead lead on your hands.

Question 153: How much is the deal worth?

There is simply no excuse for investing your organization's sustained time, effort, and energy in a person who will not share this information with your salesperson.

Question 154: In your view, what is the very next thing that has to happen for you to eventually close this sale?

Is the salesperson even thinking about a Next Step? (See Chapter Seven.)

Question 155: When and how will you make that happen?

Asking this question is basically an excuse for a group brainstorming session. Use the resource of the team's combined experience to develop ideas about how to move forward.

Question 156: Who else are they looking at?

Your salesperson should know.

Question 157: Why them?

Your salesperson should know this, too.

Question 158: What does your contact think is going to happen next?

This is perhaps the most important question of the meeting. If your salesperson thinks it's going to close this week, but admits sheepishly that this will be news to the prospect, there's a problem.

Question 159: When is that going to happen?

Demand a clear plan of action.

Question 160: Do they want this deal to happen as much as you do?

A "gut-check" question, and one that you should make a habit of asking. Keep a record of the responses, and make a point of reminding your people about what they said last week when you asked this!

Chapter Six

Questions That Move You Toward a Next Step

We have been looking at a lot of different questions that you can ask at various points during the meeting. For superior salespeople, however, asking intelligent questions at the beginning of the relationship is only part of the equation.

Assuming that our goal is to close the sale by use of a series of face-to-face meetings—which is still the model that is most relevant to most of the salespeople I work with—we will want to focus not only on gathering the right information, but also on *getting action and commitment* from the other side.

Here's the bottom line: *Don't leave this meeting without getting an appointment for the next meeting!*

Your Investment

There is really no point in investing time, energy, and attention in a relationship with a prospect if that person is not going to invest anything of consequence in return. Some people understand this principle on an intellectual level, but they fail to put that understanding into practice. How do I know? Simple. When I train salespeople and ask them how a particular prospect feels about the possibility of working with their company, I hear things like this:

- "He is very unhappy with what he is already doing. He's looking for a new vendor."
- "He called me, he is very excited, and he wants to move forward."
- "She is looking at a number of different vendors, and we are on the shortlist. I feel like we have the inside track."

These assessments, as exciting as they are to the salespeople who say them, usually wilt under close examination.

Think about it: If the person is really that "unhappy" with their current vendor, he or she should be actively engaged in the process of finding a new one, right? That's only logical. Well, if the person is actively engaged in that process, the prospect should have no problem designating a specific time and date to meet with us again! And yet, when I ask salespeople to specify when they are next scheduled to meet or speak with the person they have identified as a "hot prospect," here is what comes back:

■ "Well, I haven't got anything specific set up now . . . but I know they're going to buy."

This is completely contradictory with what the salesperson just told me!

YOUR QUESTIONING STRATEGY

Always remember this:

Interest is measured by *actions* . . . not by words!

The person cannot *both* be heavily invested in the process of working with you *and at the same time* refuse to meet with you or speak with you.

Interest really is determined by action. If the person is not interested enough to schedule a Next Step with you—and by Next Step I mean some kind of commitment to meet or speak with you at a specific date and time at some point within the next two weeks—then you should not forecast income from that lead.

Your Work Is on the Line!

It takes a lot of hard work to set a first meeting with a prospect.

It takes a lot of hard work to prepare effectively for the meeting.

It takes a lot of hard work to interview intelligently during that first face-to-face meeting.

If this is all true—and anyone who has been selling for more than a month will agree that it is—then why on earth wouldn't we strategize both a primary *and a backup* strategy for getting a Next Step before we walk in the door?

This part of the book is where the rubber hits the road. No matter how good an interviewer you are, if you are not willing to ask aggressively and directly for a Next Step from your prospect, you will not be successful as a salesperson. You may scrape by, but you will not earn a great deal of money. So, read what follows carefully—and implement it!

YOUR QUESTIONING STRATEGY

The questions that follow in this section of the book are designed to help you win commitments from your prospect *before you leave the site of that first meeting*. The Next Step you offer should be helpful to the other person, easy to agree to, and focused on a specific date and time.

You can dramatically increase your revenue and your prospects by making ONE CHANGE in your routine: Ask directly for a Next Step by proposing a *scheduled date and time for the next contact* at the conclusion of your meeting.

Practice, Not Theory!

Make sure this Next Step philosophy becomes a questioning *practice*—not just questioning theory. Make the effort. Ask the questions. Track the numbers.

One of our salespeople monitored his first appointment to second appointment ratio and found it was 7:1. He implemented the questions you're about to read, and he got that ratio down to 1.9:1—a huge improvement! (Not surprisingly, his income exploded.)

*Always, repeat, **always**, ask for a scheduled Next Step at the conclusion of a meeting with a prospect!* The following questions can help you to do that in the most effective way possible—but only if you remember to always use them!

Question 161: Can we meet next Tuesday at 2:00—so I can show you an outline of how we might be able to work together?

This is a request for an Outline Meeting. There's a very good chance this kind of meeting should be your primary Next Step option, which is why I'm featuring it prominently in this chapter.

The outline is, first and foremost, a reason to come back to meet with the prospect. As a general rule, this is the single, most effective strategy for regaining a meeting with a prospect after a face-to-face meeting. If the meeting has gone well and you have identified a potential area of benefit to the prospect, you should have no difficulties winning this particular kind of Next Step. If the meeting has not gone well, you will know, because the person will be hesitant or completely resistant to the notion of meeting with you again to discuss this outline.

Sometimes salespeople ask me, "How do I put it together? What is an outline?"

Basically, an outline is a document that says, "I am not a proposal." This is an opportunity for you to offer a condensed overview of your ideas about:

- Timing
- Pricing
- The specific products and services that could help the prospect gain the goals that you discussed together

You should practice your request for the Outline Meeting carefully. As a matter of fact, I am going to strongly suggest that you act out the end of the first meeting with a sales manager or colleague before you attempt to incorporate this question. The way you ask this question will depend on the specifics of what has gone before in your relationship with the prospect, and it will probably be different every time you pose it.

In practice, this may end up being a *longer* question than any other question you ask—because it is, in essence, the conclusion of the meeting. Here's a variation that will show you what I mean. This is how I might ask for an Outline Meeting:

Question 162: Okay, Mr. Prospect, I think we are thinking along the same lines—at least I hope we are. Here is what I want to do next. I would like to go back to my office and share what you have told me about your recruitment goals with some of the senior people at my company, and then what I want to do is brainstorm with them and give them the opportunity to share their insights on how we might be able to put together a plan for you. I don't think we are ready to look at a *proposal* yet, but what I do think we are in the position to do is show you an outline. I would like to come back here next Tuesday at 10:00 just to show you some of our initial thinking on what might go into the proposal, and then I would like to meet with some of the other people on your team who might be able to help us develop the program more fully. Does that make sense?

Whew!

It takes practice, but believe me when I tell you that you can learn to deliver this kind of question smoothly.

Did you notice how the "request" for the meeting to go over the outline appeared in the middle of all that? That is a fairly sophisticated technique, but it is one I would recommend that you practice and master. Simply asking, "Can we get together next week on Tuesday at 2:00?" will not deliver quite the same results as outlining your battle plan and incorporating the Next Step as an assumption within it.

In the best situation, what you want to do is give a verbal summary of your battle plan, with fairly detailed, comprehensive steps—and then simply ask your prospect whether or not "that makes sense." (Notice that before we can ask the ultimate question, "whether it makes sense" to buy our product or service, we have to ask ourselves whether it "makes sense" to take these preliminary steps.)

Even if you do not get the prospect to agree to meet with you again to go over your outline—you must ask the prospect to do something!

Your Questioning Strategy

When in doubt, ask the other person to do something—anything. (We will be discussing other Next Step options a little bit later in this chapter.)

Question 163: Why wouldn't you want to meet next week?

This is the all-purpose follow-through question when your request for a Next Step is shot down. If you don't know why the person doesn't want to meet with you again, you should.

Have this question ready in case you encounter resistance, tactful or otherwise, to your request for another meeting. It is best delivered, not as an indictment or an accusation, but out of an emotion of genuine surprise.

I like to deliver this question at length, and with a tone of very mild alarm that I may have committed some lapse in etiquette. Take a look:

Question 164: Wow—I am kind of surprised to hear you say that. Usually by this point in the meeting, people are very eager to meet with us again. Just out of curiosity, why wouldn't you want get together again to look at our outline?

The key, at this point, is to shut up and wait for the other person to talk. This can take discipline, because there may be an awkward silence that follows. It is imperative that you not make any attempt to fill that awkward silence.

Eventually, the person will begin to give you a clearer picture about exactly where you stand. This answer will typically begin with the words, "The thing is . . ." It is not uncommon for prospects who have held back on providing critical information—about budget, about timelines, about decision-making processes, about any number of other important aspects related to your sale—to offer them in detail at this point in the meeting.

Notice that you are asking directly for the Next Step, and then following up with a serious, nonconfrontational question, from one professional to another, about why there would be a problem in granting such a Next Step. This situation is sometimes what yields the real picture about what is going on in the organization. The point is to make the most of the capital—the time and energy you have invested—that was required to make this first meeting happen at all. You might as well use that investment to get a straight answer as to why the person does not want to meet with you again.

Questions to Use for Backup Plans

Let's look next at some good "backup" Next Steps you can ask about if you don't get the one you ask for first.

Question 165: Can I meet with your team and report back to you on (May 31)?

This is one of my favorite "backup" Next Steps. When I find myself face-to-face with a top decision-maker who, for whatever reason, does not wish to meet with me again in the short term, I will often say something like this:

"Why don't we do this, then: Let me meet with your team, let me listen to them in action, and let me take some notes. Then, when your schedule frees up, you and I can meet—let's say at the end of this month on the 31st at 2:00 P.M.—and I can debrief you on what I have learned and how we might be able to help. Does that make sense?"

If the person is not willing to work with you along these lines, it is a very good bet that you simply do not have a prospect. After all, you're basically offering to do free consulting work. *Do not make the mistake of investing vast amounts of time, energy, or attention in such a person.*

Question 166: Why don't we get my boss to meet your boss?

This is a classic "up the ante" maneuver, a great way to justify expanding the relationship and moving out of a situation where you are "stuck" with someone who has little or no decision-making authority.

You will have to pick your shot carefully, but this is a perfect example of a question you can use to escalate the sale and expand your network within the organization.

Question 167: Why don't I set up a conference call so you can talk to one of our customers?

There is a long and storied history of winning new customers by encouraging them to talk to old ones. These days, it is not necessary to go to all the trouble of arranging an actual face-to-face meeting. It is far easier, and a good deal speedier, to simply set up a conference call. Just remember that the conclusion of the call, like the conclusion of the first meeting, should include a clear request for a slot on the prospect's calendar, preferably within the next two weeks.

Question 168: Why don't you come to one of our company events?

This can be a training seminar, a trade show, an investor meeting, a company celebration, a holiday party, or even an event you design specifically for the benefit of this one contact. The closer the theme of the event is to your contact's business goals or key concerns, obviously, the more likely you will be to get him or her to agree to attend.

Here, as with every Next Step request, your goal is to make it easy for the person to say "yes." Do not make the mistake of encouraging the person to come, and then charging him or her an arm and a leg to do so. Ideally, the event should be free.

Question 169: Why don't you come take a look at our facility?

This can be an office, a manufacturing plant, a display room, or any other location that seems relevant to your business and will show your company in the best light. Sometimes, you can win a Next Step that involves your boss more easily by scheduling a time for the prospect to "drop by the office" and "happen" to meet your superior. Whatever works.

Question 170: Can I get a tour of your facility?

This is another classic "backup" to the request for a meeting to go over the outline. If the person with whom you wish to meet legitimately does not have any slot in which to meet you over the next two weeks, why on earth would he or she deny you the opportunity to see the operation up close?

Ask to take a look at the plant floor. Ask to take a look at the showroom. Ask to take a look at the sales office. Ask to take a look at *anything* . . . just make sure it involves someone in the prospect's network, and try to set a date when you can report back on your findings.

Question 171: Why don't I come back and show you . . . ?

How you finish the sentence is up to you, but it should have something to do with seeing your product or service in action.

If you sell software, offer to come back and show the prospect a demo version of the particular program you think might match his or her situation. If you sell promotional items, offer to bring back a variety of samples so that your prospect can take a look at some of the most likely matches with his or her organization. If you sell consulting, offer to come back with a demonstration of what has worked well for other clients in the past.

Again, make sure that the date you are asking for occurs at some point within the next two weeks. *If the Next Step is scheduled for further than two weeks out, it is significantly less likely to take place.* (Think about it—isn't it easier for you to make a halfhearted "commitment" for a slot that's a month away than for next Friday?)

Question 172: Why don't I do an online presentation for your key people?

Not my favorite Next Step, but infinitely preferable to the common sales mistake of simply saying "yes" when a prospect asks you to put together a PowerPoint presentation for his or her team.

Consider all the likely downsides for simply complying with this request.

- You spend the better part of a day, or perhaps even more, developing a flashy PowerPoint presentation.
- You e-mail the PowerPoint to your contact.
- Nothing happens.
- You call back to check in. Your prospect promises to call and let you know what people thought of the PowerPoint.
- Nothing happens.

Perhaps your contact shows your labor of love to all the key people on the team, but then again, perhaps the e-mail sits unopened for a week or more. And then what do you do?

Far better, and far more revealing of the true state of the relationship, is to ask for an opportunity to deliver the presentation *yourself*, and to discuss it with *all* the key people during a conference call. After all, you're a salesperson. This is the sort of thing salespeople do.

It is very important to remember that you are engaging in a transaction here. You are trading your work, research efforts, and the expertise of yourself and your staff and your organization for attention, interaction, and meaningful feedback. You are not paid to do this work in a vacuum, and you should not agree to do so.

Question 173: Why don't we set a time now to debrief about the online presentation?

I strongly recommend that before you deliver your online presentation to the group, you work with your contact to set up a day and time for debriefing, either by phone or in person. If you cannot do that, and there is no reason you should not, you can conclude the presentation with a call to action of some kind: "So, what do people think? Can we start on May 12?"

I should reiterate, perhaps, that I am not particularly fond of online presentations when it is possible to arrange for a face-to-face meeting. Even so, there are situations where it is the most plausible and meaningful Next Step—for instance, when a CEO is in Missouri and your contact is in Sacramento, and your contact is, in fact, eager to have a discussion with you and the CEO at the same time.

There are any number of quality presentation options available online now, and most of them are quite affordable. Although this should not be your first option for a Next Step, it is probably something that should be in your repertoire.

Question 174: Why don't you and I meet with my boss?

If you have the opportunity, bringing up your superior—whether it is a sales manager, division vice-president, or even the CEO of the company—is a great way to get the prospect involved in the sales cycle, and to agree to meet with you for a second time. Obviously, you will have to evaluate the potential importance of the deal before deciding to lobby for your manager to attend the next meeting.

Question 175: Why don't you and I meet with our technical expert? *Or* Why don't we get your technical people together with my technical people?

The first question can refer to a Web designer, a design specialist, an architect, a safety engineer, or any of a hundred other people who possess specialized knowledge that is relevant to your prospect's world.

The second question can be another effective strategy for bringing other people into the mix. If your prospect is resistant to the idea of bringing other people into the next meeting, consider asking . . .

Question 176: How do you (upload your two-dimensional widget projections)?

Otherwise known as "the question they can't answer."

As a sales professional, I like to follow two rules: 1) Ask for explanations about every technical term that came your way that you did not understand, and 2) be sure that the prospect understands everything you said about your own company's products and services.

The present question does not exactly *break* either of those rules, but it is something of a creative "work-around" meant for use in situations where you need a Next Step with someone other than your current contact. It employs a certain "strategic incomprehensibility," if you will, in pursuing that goal.

By asking a question that you know your contact will be unable to answer, you highlight a reason to get access to someone else in the organization: you need this information to build your eventual proposal!

How It Works

Let's say that you know for a fact that your product or service will require the use of two-dimensional widget projections. And let's say, for the sake of argument, that you also know that your contact has absolutely no experience with this particular aspect of widget maintenance. Finally, let's assume that the person you are talking to really has no internal authority within the organization, and cannot give any meaningful information about how to move forward within a given timeline or specify any dollar amount or budget that the company is willing to invest in your product or service.

You have two choices, only one of which is good. You could decide to continue scheduling meetings with this person, even though you have basically hit a dead end. Or, you could find some ingenious way of moving up to interact with someone else in the organization. The question strategy I am outlining here is a proven method for doing just that.

By asking in a polite but persistent way about some technical or internal aspect of your contact's world that he or she simply cannot answer, you know that you are highly likely to generate a response that sounds like this: "I really have no idea." And that is exactly what you are after. When you hear that, you can say, "Well, it is going to be pretty important for us to figure out all the details about the widget projection; maybe I could speak to the head of the widget-uploading department next week with you. Why don't we go over to his area now and see if we can set up a time for us all to get together?"

This is a tactful and utterly fair way to use our own insight and intelligence to move the sales cycle forward. Notice, however, that even though we are asking a question that we know the person cannot answer, we are not spending large amounts of time throwing technical terminology at the person. We're posing *one* question whose answer will require us to interact with someone else in the company.

Question 177: What do you think we should do next?

Not as dumb a question as it sounds . . . assuming you're talking to the right person.

If you're dealing with the owner, CEO, president, or some other top banana, this can be an excellent Next Step question. These folks live to give instructions. Let them.

An effective variation is:

Question 178: Whom do you want me to talk to next?

Again, only for use with a high-level executive. It can be quite startlingly effective. ("I want you to call Jim Miller in Accounting and come up with an action plan by next Wednesday morning.")

If you use this approach, be sure to ask:

Question 179: Can I keep you in the loop?

Once you secure a high-level internal referral as a Next Step, make sure the senior executive knows you'll be copying him on everything you do. If you run into a snag, this person may be able to help you overcome it.

And If You Can't Get a Next Step . . .

Question 180: Is there someone else in your industry whom you think I should be talking to?

When in doubt, ask for referrals. (Actually, you should ask for referrals anyway, whether or not you get a Next Step!)

Chapter Seven

"Next Step" Questions for Managers Only

The same principles we covered in Chapter Six apply here. If you make a habit of asking these questions every week, then your salespeople will make a habit of having the right answers for you.

Question 181: Do you have enough first appointments?

Establish a minimum quota for the salesperson to have at all times. *This quota is more important than the sales quota you set for the week, month, or quarter!*

For a full discussion of ratios and first appointment quotas, see my book *Cold Calling Techniques (That Really Work!)*.

Question 182: How many of your meetings this week are taking place within the time frame of your average selling cycle?

Remember, the longer the discussion goes beyond the person's average selling cycle, the less likely the deal is to close. Be ruthless with salespeople who spend all their time and energy setting Next Steps with people who are in "permanent pending" mode.

Question 183: How many *new* prospects do you have for this week as compared to last week?

Is the person coasting on past contacts? If so, prescribe more prospecting calls! (See Chapter Two.)

Question 184: Is your activity in balance?

In other words, is there a balance between this representative's new accounts vs. existing accounts, and between big accounts vs. smaller accounts?

Question 185: In scheduling your next week's activity, what is the best territory management approach?

What key prospects/customers can the salesperson schedule meetings with who are near people he or she has already made a commitment to meet?

Question 186: Who can I call for you?

Ask yourself: "How can I, the manager, get involved in these sales?" Don't be afraid to call up a "fifty-fifty" prospect and say, "I hear we're going to be doing business together!" You will quickly learn *exactly* where your salesperson actually stands with this prospect.

Question 187: What is your goal for the next meeting with this person?

What, specifically, is the salesperson trying to accomplish?

Question 188: How will you open the next meeting?

Does the salesperson have a plan for the next meeting? Who else within your organization does it involve?

Question 189: What Next Step strategy will you use to get back?

A trick question. You actually want the salesperson to tell you not only about his or her *primary* Next Step strategy, but also the backup strategy.

Chapter Eight

Questions That Help You Identify and Deliver the Right Presentation

Asking for—and getting—the Next Step is a big part of the equation for high-level sales success. But it's not the only part of the equation.

In this part of the book, you get a look at questions that will help you confirm that you really are on the right track—*and* lay the foundation for the presentation that will win you the deal.

The Presentation

There is a lot of advice out there regarding how to deliver a sales presentation. Much of this information focuses on basic but important issues like establishing eye contact, using effective body language, developing rapport with the individual or group, and setting up snazzy PowerPoint graphics.

All of these are important issues, but they are not as important as identifying and verifying and developing the information that will lead you to a recommendation that will make sense from the other side's point of view.

The Secret of Withholding

One of the secrets to high achievement in sales, in my experience, lies in withholding one's presentation until the right information has been verified. For my part, I am much more inclined to hold off doing a presentation altogether until I am relatively certain that the person with whom I am working will in fact buy it.

The questions that follow are designed to help you get to this point with your prospect, whether you are talking to an individual or a group. Do not attempt to make a presentation until you have covered all or most of the issues addressed in this chapter! If you follow this advice, you will *verify* your information, as we discussed in Chapter One, prepare and deliver *fewer* presentations, spend more of your time with live leads, and have a far higher closing ratio than the average salesperson.

What makes more sense—delivering five customized proposals to five prospects who really are "playing ball" with you, and who have helped you to develop your presentation— or delivering twenty-five UNCUSTOMIZED proposals that have little or nothing to do with what people are trying to accomplish?

Never make a presentation that you do not think will close!

A Word about "Presentation Tricks"

What you're about to read will not give you much guidance on the question of what color graphics to use, how to make images zoom around, how to evaluate group dynamics, or how to tell when someone is bored with what you are doing. These topics have been examined in depth in a hundred other books on selling, and a twenty-minute visit to the World Wide Web can point you toward resources that will help you out.

What you won't find on the Internet, however, are the questions that allow you to confirm that the content of the presentations you are planning to deliver will really result in a sale. That's what follows. Use it!

Question 190: Before we get started, can I share with you what I got from our last meeting?

This is one of many possible variations on a "verifying" question. I like to begin the "business portion" of the second meeting with a question like this, because it allows me to restate the key points that I gathered from the initial meeting, and to move into a side-by-side review of an important sales document: the outline.

An outline is a one-page or two-page summary of how you might be able to work with this person, based on what you got from the prospect during your last meeting. Its goal is not to sell, but to encourage the prospect to take part in direct revision.

What I usually do is pull the outline from my briefcase when I ask this question. I then revisit all the key points that I "got from our last conversation," and elicit direct input from the prospect by stopping after each point and saying something like

"Here are my assumptions," followed by questions that sound like the following:

The phrase "Before we begin" is a very nearly perfect transition phrase—in this case, for the beginning of a second or subsequent meeting. The phrase helps you move from the small-talk portion of the meeting into the "business" portion of the meeting without any difficulty—and actually marks the "beginning" of the reason for your visit, even though it pretends not to.

Question 191: Before we begin, can I share what I discussed with my boss/team/manager about our last meeting?

A variation on Question 190. I recommend you use this question to begin your second or subsequent meeting for two reasons. First, use it because this portion of the meeting is extremely important, and this opening is an easy and effective way to begin it; and second, use it because you *must* draw your prospect into a direct discussion of the assumptions you gathered the first time through. This question increases your chances of doing just that.

There is perhaps no more critical moment in the sale than when your prospect decides whether or not he is going to offer an in-depth revision of your ideas. If you get this kind of insight, and you are speaking with someone who has real decision-making authority within the organization, you will in all likelihood win the sale. If you do not get this kind of input, your odds are considerably lower that you will ever see income for your efforts.

Many salespeople misunderstand the role of this question. It is not to get the prospect to "agree" with everything that has gone before or to encourage him or her to "pitch" the outline you have developed to others in the organization. In fact, you are trying to *get the person to tell you what does not work about your recap.*

Assuming you have had one face-to-face meeting, and you are currently presenting these ideas during the second face-to-face meeting, it would be remarkable if everything in your outline actually did match up with the prospect's current state of mind. For one thing, remember that the quality of information rises as the number of contacts increases. So even if you have a "great" meeting during the first face-to-face encounter, you should expect to find new and better information during the second meeting. If you don't, you're in trouble.

So use this question—and understand its purpose. This is the point at which you share with the prospect the specifics of the outline you put together—and then stop talking to see whether or not she will start revising the document on your behalf. Once the person takes ownership of the outline, she is very likely to take ownership of the project as a whole.

Question 192: Has anything changed since our last meeting?

An extremely important question and one that should be part of any second meeting. I cannot tell you the number of times I have spoken to salespeople who swore that absolutely nothing of consequence had changed between the first and second meeting—only to tell me later that the competition had somehow wormed its way into the account.

Look the person straight in the eye—not threateningly, but with genuine interest—and pose this question. Stop talking. See what happens.

Question 193: Did you have a chance to talk to anyone else in the organization about what we discussed last time?

This question brings up an underexamined issue within the sales process—and a vitally important subject for the second meeting.

Maybe your prospect has been circulating your ideas around the target organization; maybe not. Either situation is worth examining; either will affect the way that your second meeting proceeds.

If the person has been discussing your initiatives with others in the organization, you will certainly want to know what the feedback was and who is "in the loop."

Pose the question earnestly and with curiosity, and find out what is happening by using the most effective rhetorical "weapon" of them all—silence.

Question 194: Just to get some feedback on this outline, why don't you and I set up a meeting/conference call with . . . ?

This question assumes that the answer to Question 191 is "no," *and* your prospect can't get the decision made for you, *and* you're approaching the end of the meeting.

If the person has made no effort whatsoever to bounce your ideas off the other people in the organization, you should try to find a way to help him or her do the bouncing before you conclude this meeting: perhaps a conference call, perhaps a group meeting, perhaps an impromptu swing by the boss's office right then and there. Could it hurt to ask?

Question 195: Are we thinking along the same lines in terms of price?

Verify the dollars: Offer a specific price or, alternatively, a price range for a variety of possible offerings. *Get a reaction before moving on.*

Question 196: Is this product/service what you are looking for?

Verify that the product/service offering really does make sense to the other person. *Get a reaction before moving on.*

Question 197: Have I got the timing about right?

Verify the timing: Be specific about the delivery or rollout schedule. *Get a reaction before moving on.*

By specifying timing ("I think we could start next month"), you will usually get some kind of reaction from the prospect!

If you don't—if you sense hesitation, but the person does not offer specific changes or feedback, say . . .

Question 198: I'm sensing that there is a problem somewhere—where did I go off track?

Stop talking! Wait until you get a response.

You cannot verify your information without feedback from the prospect.

As we have seen, this "verification" step is an extremely important concept, and is one of the more important and frequently ignored areas of sales questioning. We must be willing to elicit new facts from a prospect, and to confirm that the information we got last time really is correct. Even if posing a question like this feels awkward, *that awkwardness is better than investing more time in the relationship without specific guidance from the prospect.* These are essential preliminaries to the presentation; if we simply rush forward to deliver our presentation, we may miss the mark.

Use this question, and your outline, to bring out objections and issues in a "safe environment"—while you are still in the interviewing phase.

Verified or Not?

How will we know when we are done with the verification step? It is actually very easy to tell. If we are still in active discussions with a prospect—in other words, if he or she is still willing to schedule a Next Step to meet again with us within the next two weeks—and if we have a sense that we are "in the ballpark" with regard to timing, pricing, and the specific product and service in question, then we can assume that our information has been verified. What we are basically doing during the verification stage is asking the prospect: Here is what I am planning to recommend—do you think it will work?

Do not be afraid to offer specifics. On the other hand, don't throw a thirty-page document at the prospect as a means of "verification." The goal is to get a single piece of paper, or at the most two sheets of paper, that outline your thinking and all the key elements.

Question 199: I feel as if I'm missing something—what do you think I'm missing here?

This is another question that can be very helpful when you're dealing with a decision-maker who is interested in moving the relationship forward with you, but has not provided much in the way of meaningful feedback about the outline you are using to develop your proposal.

When in doubt, say that you feel as though you have made a mistake or oversight, and ask for a correction.

Some salespeople do not verify their information because they are afraid of making a mistake in front of the prospect. They should be afraid of investing a week or more of their time in developing a proposal for someone that does not match that person's world! The key to improving your closing ratios lies in your willingness to be corrected by the other person. If you are never corrected by your prospects, guess what? You are not asking the right questions!

Make sure that you conduct the verification phase of your sales process with the right demeanor. Your goal is to come across as an ally who has a couple of questions and needs some guidance, not as a private detective or, worse, a prosecuting attorney. If you never get any clarifying or corrective feedback from your prospects, you may want to step back and look at why this is so. You may be intimidating people or you may be trying to move forward in the sales cycle too quickly. Do the responses you get tend to become shorter and shorter, and contain less meaningful information, as the relationship progresses? If so, you need to work on your willingness to be corrected!

Always remember, you want the prospect to "right" your "wrong." When your prospect corrects you—you win!

Question 200: That's how I would put what we're trying to do—but how would you put it?

Use this question to draw out a less-than talkative prospect and to identify specific terminology that should be incorporated in your final proposal.

I have a simple principle that I like to follow when it comes to building proposals: *They must be written or dictated by the prospect, at least in part.*

If you're not incorporating the prospect's terminology for the proposal, there's a problem. You don't have to sell for very long to realize that there are certain internal terms and phrases that resonate well within the target organization. The problem is that when you are opening the relationship, you do not really know what those words and phrases are, nor do you know what key issues are driving the decision-maker. This question may help to illuminate things. Take notes on the answer you hear.

Do not underestimate the importance of identifying specific key words that will motivate and energize a prospect. I have closed more than one sale by noticing a person's change in demeanor when a certain word comes up in a discussion, often as a result of this question. Make sure you write down these words. Examples of such words might include, "margin," "retention," "market share," "expansion"—they'll be different for every situation. Find out what they are for *your* prospect and build them into your proposal.

Question 201: Just between you and me, what do you really think is going to happen here?

This is among the most important sales questions of them all—but you have to know *when* and *how* to ask it.

If you ask it during the body of the second meeting, you may or may not get the straight scoop. And you may get a long monologue that serves as more of a distraction than anything else.

If, on the other hand, you were to wait until the "business" portion of the meeting is over, make all the small talk, shake hands, and let your prospect walk you to the door . . . and *then* pose this question, you will get a direct, honest assessment of exactly where you are in the sales cycle. You might even get the "inside information" you need to complete the deal.

Try it!

YOUR QUESTIONING STRATEGY

Your goal with these kinds of questions is to focus on, fine-tune, and eventually formalize the recommendation that really does match up with the goals and objectives that are foremost in your prospect's mind.

Sales and Leadership

During my training programs, I often emphasize the fact that leadership in selling, and in business as a whole, can be understood as the ability to say "follow me" and have other people do just that. In order to say follow me, and be followed, it is vitally important for the person aspiring to the leadership role to take into account what the other person is trying to accomplish.

Even a military officer who has formal "authority" over the soldiers in his unit will quickly find that a strategy of issuing orders that lead only to disaster, mayhem, and death will undermine his "authority" very quickly. People decide to follow, and risk their lives, fortunes, and careers based on their assessment that the person they are following really does have their best interests at heart. Use the following questions in this chapter to confirm that what you recommend really does meet that standard, and to confirm that you are truly dealing with a prospect who is willing to seriously consider investing money in your product or service.

Dealing with Committees

It is quite common for our request for a Next Step to meet with the following response: "Let me bounce this off the so-and-so committee (or: such-and-such a work group) and see what they have to say about it."

Or:

"I'll have to run this past the committee—they make all the decisions in this area."

Or:

"It looks good—we just need to get approval from the committee, but don't worry, that's just a formality."

In all three situations, your first response should be to ask the following question directly:

Question 202: Can I make a presentation directly to the committee (team/work group)?

The number of salespeople who fail to ask this basic sales question is deeply disturbing!

The committee is meeting to discuss your initiative, or to determine the best way to select a vendor in your area. Why on earth wouldn't you want to speak in front of this group? And yet, far too many salespeople will follow the prospect's lead and accept a passive role, because the prospect says "that is how we have always done it."

Remember, you are an agent of change as a salesperson, and it is in your interest—and the prospect's interest—to propose new and imaginative ways of doing things. Ask directly for the opportunity to make your case before the committee.

If you don't receive authorization to make a presentation before the committee, you should ask:

Question 203: I'm surprised to hear you say that. Why wouldn't you want me to talk before the committee (team/ work group)?

Take careful notes on the answer you hear. If there is still some hidden obstacle, you may well get the straight story at this point. *But you must ask this question in order to identify what the obstacle is!*

Follow through with appropriate "how" and "why" questions.

If possible, position yourself as a resource to the prospect. Offer to lessen his or her workload by doing the work of preparing for and delivering the presentation ahead of time.

If, on the other hand, you *do* receive the go-ahead to deliver your presentation before the committee (which will happen more often than not if you're really looking at a live prospect), don't just set the date and excuse yourself until the day of the meeting. There's quite a lot of preparatory work to do, and you should be sure to ask *all* of the following questions.

Question 204: What can you tell me about how the committee works?

This is a good initial discussion point with your contact and will help you get your bearings. Do not agree to any course of action before you explore the nature and role of the committee with your contact. You will want to strategize what follows very carefully, and you are going to need your contact's insights in order to do so.

This is an open-ended question. Very often, it will give you the essential "ground rules" of the group's working process. Be prepared to follow up with specific questions, such as:

Question 205: How will the final decision be made after the committee meets?

You are only likely to get a straight, reliable answer from the prospect once he or she has invested a significant amount of effort in the relationship with your firm. It's best to hold this question until the second or subsequent meeting if you can.

Question 206: Who would we be presenting to?

Identify as much as you possibly can about the nature and roles of the people on the committee. Try to find out where the agendas are, and who is likely to be the "tie-breaker" in the event that the committee splits down the middle.

Question 207: How was the committee formed?

Another way of posing this important question is:

Question 208: When did the committee first meet?

With both Question 207 and Question 208, your aim is to find out the specifics—the genealogy, if you will, of the group you'll be presenting to. Is this a standing committee, or has it been assembled specifically for the purpose of evaluating your products and services and those of your competitors? The motives and objectives of one group will be very different from those of another. If the committee has been formed recently, you will want to try to get help in reaching out to the person who formed the committee, even if he or she does not have a role on the committee itself. This person is likely to be the final decision-maker, and it is definitely in your interest to try to secure a meeting.

Question 209: How should we reach out to the people on the committee?

Your goal in dealing with the committee is not to walk in unprepared, but rather to do the necessary work *up-front* to reach out to all the members of the group before your meeting. This may mean a long series of phone calls, e-mails, and even face-to-face meetings before your committee presentation. Only you can determine whether this investment of time and effort is worth it. However, in deals that carry high price tags, it is quite common for a committee to deliver the final recommendation, and it may well be worth identifying the key players and discussing their priorities ahead of time.

Keep your contact in the loop on all your discussions, unless you have a good strategic reason for doing otherwise.

Question 210: Can you and I set up a time to debrief right now?

The point here is to secure the Next Step with your prospect *before* you actually make your presentation to the committee. Question 210 is extremely important—be sure you ask it before you start investing the time necessary to develop your presentation! If the prospect is unwilling to schedule a time to meet with you after the meeting, there is a very good chance that there is some deal-killing obstacle or difficulty that you have not yet uncovered.

Let's say it's March 1. The committee is meeting on March 15, and you will be making your presentation to them at that point. It is incumbent upon you, *right now*, to set up a Next Step with your prospect—and schedule a meeting with him, or with someone else in the organization, to debrief on how the committee meeting went. That meeting might be scheduled for, say, March 17.

What you do *not* want to do is allow the meeting to conclude without some kind of Next Step in your prospect's calendar.

Remember, this is a series of exchanges. You are trading your knowledge, insights, and expertise for ongoing commitments of time and attention. Do not invest heavily without receiving a parallel investment from the other side.

Question 211: What do you think (person *X*) will think about what we've put together?

If you can, you should pose this question about every committee member you are able to identify.

Question 212: How many good copies should I put together/bring?

A good way of determining the number of people on the committee, if for some reason your prospect has been vague about it up to this point.

Question 213: Just between you and me, what do you think the result of the meeting is going to be?

A question best asked "informally," near the end of your meeting with the prospect. (See Question 201.)

Now—let's assume that the prospect really is interested in moving forward in the sales process with you, but for some legitimate reason can't manage to get you in front of the group to make the presentation yourself. (Perhaps the "committee" is a formal gathering, such as the annual meeting of a board of directors, and outsiders are not allowed.) In this situation, you should still ask:

Question 214: Can I build the presentation for you?

Or . . .

Question 215: Can I put together a first draft of the presentation for you?

This question comes in two flavors; use Question 215 for those prospects who are born "tweakers." (Let's face it, some people live to revise and improve other people's work.)

The point is to get *some* kind of input into what will actually be discussed at the meeting. Building the PowerPoint deck for your prospect (or its initial draft) is an excellent way to do this.

You should also volunteer to put together the agenda and any other support materials for the meeting.

Do not rely on your prospect's memory of your proposal to guide his or her discussions before the committee. Let's face it, sometimes things do get lost in translation. (One of our company's trainers has a saying that encapsulates this fact of business life concisely and accurately: "People barely communicate.")

A Presentation Checklist

Do not deliver your formal presentation to the prospect until you can answer YES to all of the following questions:

- Are you talking to the right person—the actual decision-maker or the person who can get the decision made for you?
- Does the plan you are preparing to put forward make sense from the other person's side, given what you have learned about what this person and this organization are trying to accomplish?
- Does this person agree with your pricing?
- Does this person agree with your timetable? (Is there a specific date for implementation/start-up/switchover? What is it?)
- Have you prepared success stories that will help the prospect visualize the benefit of working with you?
- Have you verified your information?
- Does your plan/proposal use VERBATIM feedback based on notes you've taken during discussions with the prospect?
- Does this person KNOW that you intend to close the sale at the next meeting?

A single "no" answer to any of these questions means you are not ready to make a formal recommendation to do business with this prospect.

Chapter Nine

Questions That Deal with Setbacks or Obstacles in the Sales Process

Inevitably, we face obstacles or challenges in the sales process. That is only natural. If we did not face these challenges, we would not be salespeople, but rather customer service representatives.

Lots of salespeople ask me to share questions and strategies that will allow them to "overcome objections." I'll be honest—I really don't like the term *objections*. It's better to think of them as responses.

Think about it. When someone tells you there's a problem with what you're suggesting, that at least shows that the person is actually listening and thinking about your products and services. That means you have the opportunity to advance the sale by asking questions, by getting "righted," and then putting a spotlight on your organization's relevant resources.

Responses from the prospect give us the opportunity to gain insight on what the other person is thinking. Try to ask questions that will help you get to the bottom of whatever the prospect is trying to draw your attention to.

Remember: ANY feedback from the prospect is a form of "getting righted."

Resolving the Issues

Often, we hear a negative response and assume that it is an objection, especially when it concerns price. In many cases, the prospect has simply raised an issue that needs to be explored. Price concerns often mask other issues.

Before you proceed to the questions in this chapter, I'd like to ask you to take just a moment to think of the last time you bought an appliance, like a stereo or a television. What happened? Perhaps you walked into the store having decided that you wouldn't spend more than, say, $750. Sometimes we give the store attendant a particular price range, and he or she points us toward a particular model. Then we find ourselves bombarded with reasons that model is perfect for us. Suddenly we're turned off.

Haven't there been other times, though, when the salesperson shared asked a couple of key questions, shared a couple of relevant stories, and emphasized a couple of key benefits … and you decided to buy even though the figure was higher than you had hoped for?

The truth of the matter is that an intelligent salesperson

who asks the right questions and doesn't overreact to initial resistance can change your "I'm only spending $750" mindset into a "$950 actually seems like a pretty good price" mindset in a matter of minutes. Haven't you ever had an experience like that before? I know I have.

To turn initial resistance into a positive response, you'll need to follow these steps:

1. IDENTIFY/ISOLATE the issues. How is this particular issue affecting this particular prospect, right now? Get the specifics. What's *behind* the person's response?
2. VALIDATE the issue. Find out what its real-world dimensions are. Talk things through frankly with your prospect. (For instance: "You know what? This is the point in the conversation where this issue comes up a lot.")
3. RESOLVE the issue. If you stop and think about it, you'll realize you really do tend to face the same half-dozen or so challenges over and over again. Choose the six most relevant success stories and share them. Use all the resources of your organization to develop a creative solution.

Questions for Identifying Issues

Question 216: Just out of curiosity . . . what makes you think that's the right figure/date/deal?

Or . . .

Question 217: What makes you say that?

Or . . .

Question 218: What were you expecting?

Remember, as sales reps, we often overreact when we hear an initial "objection." What we should be doing is giving the other person the chance to identify the problem (if there is one) and help us get to the bottom of it . . . *before* we commit to solving it. For example, if the prospect says, "The pricing isn't what I expected," don't just say, "Stop! Let me tell you why this is a great price!" or "I can ONLY cut it by 50 percent!"

(By the way, I've heard *both* of these "turnarounds" offered by seemingly rational salespeople when they heard about a tenth of a second's worth of price resistance from a prospect.)

It might make more sense to explore the issue further by asking, "What were you expecting?" Your prospect might respond by saying, "Well, so-and-so told me he paid *X*." By the same token, the prospect might say, "Well, I really didn't have any expectation, because I've never worked with a company like yours before."

These are two totally different frames of reference! STEP BACK and ask more clarifying questions. Find out what's really going on.

Question 219: Can I tell you how we handled this issue when I worked with Company *X*?

A classic get-back-on-track question. Use it!

The prospect says, "It's just too expensive."

Instead of offering to discount, you say, "What makes you think it's too expensive?"

The prospect says, "I have only *X* dollars in the budget for this—I can't touch another penny until next quarter."

You say, "Can I tell you how we handled this issue when I worked with XYZ bank? They agreed to pay *X* upfront, and we billed them 120 days later for the balance. It was no problem."

If the solution makes sense to the other person—you're in business. If there's another problem, keep cool, try to find out what it is, and offer another relevant success story.

Your Questioning Strategy

Remember—the more relevant success stories you have, the easier it will be for you to deal with obstacles in the sales cycle.

Question 220: Did I do something wrong here?

This is the biggie. Use it when you have put a lot of work into the proposal—and you feel as though the prospect has, too—but you're suddenly running into a brick wall that has no name or description, and didn't seem to exist yesterday.

Your goal is to find out what's really happening, of course. Ultimately, you will recall our closing strategy is based on recommending what "makes sense" to the other person, and then asking directly whether or not it makes sense. Our classic formulation for this is, "It makes sense to me . . . what do you think?"

In this situation, you honestly *thought* you had something that made sense from the other person's point of view, but you find out now that you don't. What's missing? What has really changed that the other person hasn't told you about? This question is your best bet for filling these mysterious information gaps.

In practice, it can be brief, as above. My suggestion,

though, is that you practice it and deliver a slightly more elaborate version, as I have outlined below, and tailor the longer version to the specific situations you face.

Question 221: Mr. Prospect, I have to be honest with you. Something is wrong here. Usually, when I have gotten this far through the process of meeting with someone, people are very excited about what I have recommended, and they do, in fact, decide to work with us. Actually, I pride myself on not making a recommendation until I am really sure that the other person is more excited about it than I am. I know for a fact that we have got the best program for you, and that it will deliver the results that you and I spoke about. So, I have to assume that I have done something wrong in outlining this plan for you. So help me out. Did I do something wrong? If I did—what was it?

Obviously, this takes a little longer to practice than Question 220, but I think you will find it is worth the effort. If you ask this question honestly and without sarcasm, you will usually get the "straight dope" on what's gone wrong, typically preceded by the words, "No, you didn't do anything wrong. You see the thing is . . . "

It is entirely possible that your sudden reversal of fortune within the sales process is the result of some higher individual within the target organization taking control of the process. If that is the case, you have a right to lay all your cards on the table and ask directly for an opportunity to make your case to that senior decision-maker.

Variants on the "Did I do something wrong?" approach can be employed at different points throughout the sales cycle. Just be sure not to overuse it, and not to employ the "full apology" I have outlined here more than once. For instance, a slightly less abject version of the apology and request for correction might come earlier in the process, and it might sound like this:

Question 222: You know, usually, by this point in my meeting with somebody, I get a lot more interaction and a lot more excitement about what I am discussing. And I get the feeling I really have not done that with you today. Did I do something wrong?

Notice that what you are really asking for here is the opportunity to find out *why* the person is not excited about what you're discussing. This is basically another attempt to "get righted."

Question 223: Did (name) do something wrong?

All too often, in sales, we do not get an outright rejection. It might be easier if we did, but what we are faced with is something nowhere near as clear-cut as that. Someone simply drops off the radar screen. We have one meeting, and it goes well. We have another meeting that also seems to go well. By the third meeting, perhaps, we are convinced that we are looking at something that really does make sense. And then . . . silence. Phone calls do not get returned, e-mails do not get answered, and attempts to set up another face-to-face meeting go nowhere.

This question, one of the most effective at resuscitating a deal that you will find, is the perfect appeal to a sense of fairness. However, it relies upon the role of another person, typically your colleague or superior, to deliver its (often spectacular) results.

How It Works

The "trick" of this question, to the degree that there is a "trick," is that it is not you, but your sales manager or colleague who calls the prospect who has suddenly become inaccessible. The message that your superior or colleague leaves should sound something like this:

"Hi, Jack. This is Mel Ryan of the ABC Company. I'm calling you regarding Dave Miller, our salesperson. Would you please give me a call back as soon as possible?"

Now, let's say that you are Dave Ryan, and that your prospect has gone for two or three weeks without returning your phone calls or answering your e-mails, or responding in any way to your correspondence. Something looked like it was about to happen, then all of the sudden, your prospect seems to vanish off the face of the earth. Assuming that your prospect has not, in fact, been abducted by aliens, he will, 95 times out of 100, immediately return the call to the sales manager or colleague who left the message.

Why? Because he feels, deep down in his heart, just a little bit guilty about having left you at the altar. When your prospect returns the call dutifully, as he is overwhelmingly likely to do, the conversation will proceed along the following lines.

Your superior: Hey, thanks for calling back. I was just calling about Dave Ryan, I know he met with you a while back, and he said that he had a couple of good meetings. Then, he said that something went wrong, and I just wanted to call up and find out if Jim had done something inappropriate, something I should know about.

Your prospect (instantly): Oh, no. He didn't do anything wrong. He did a great job. I really liked him a lot, and he did everything on earth that he should have done. The thing is . . .

At this point, right after those revealing words, "The thing is," your prospect will share with your colleague or supervisor the *real* story that he or she was reluctant to share with you. Perhaps it is a budget problem. Perhaps it's a timing issue. Perhaps it is the fact that the CEO's brother slid a competing bid in just under the deadline. Perhaps it is simple inertia, such as the fact that your prospect was supposed to complete some paperwork and has been swamped and has been unable to do so. There are any number of possible explanations for why the sale suddenly seemed to evaporate. *Your boss or colleague just needs to find out which is in play and then ask earnestly for a Next Step to address the problem.*

The point is, with this strategy, you will, at least, know exactly what is happening in the relationship. And, if your colleague or supervisor is at all on the ball, both you and your prospect and your internal partner will be having a meeting soon to discuss whether or not there is anything that can be done to rectify whatever went wrong and/or move the sales process forward. This Next Step is comparatively easy to secure. All your colleague or sales manager has to say is:

"Actually, we faced a very similar situation when we worked with the ACME Corporation. Here's what we were able to do for them . . . (and here, your ally supplies all the relevant details of the success story with ACME.) You and I and Dave should get together again next Tuesday at 2:00 to see if we can think creatively and address this problem for you."

A final note: We train salespeople to swap leads that have fallen off the radar screen, and to use this strategy to set up new meetings. What have you got to lose?

Questions for Specific Sales Obstacles

The questioning ideas will help you identify what's really going on in just about any selling situation that involves a sales obstacle or challenge. Of course, you may wish to target your questions more specifically.

Below, you'll find some more narrowly focused questions for specific challenges you may face.

Question 224: I get the feeling you are not really happy with what I've proposed here. Am I right?

Use this for prospects who are noncommittal about the formal proposal you've developed. You may also want to use this question if you feel uncomfortable for any reason with the "Did I do something wrong" question or its variations.

Question 225: Let me ask you something—by what point in time are you trying to achieve (*X*)?

Use this for situations where the prospect has agreed on everything but the timeline, which is perpetually vague for some reason.

Your aim is to find out whether the inability to commit to a specific schedule is the result of some as-yet-unidentified problem, or whether the person you are talking to simply has not thought through the logistics. If it is the latter, this question will help put you back on track. By asking, for instance . . .

Question 226: When do you want your new stores to be open to the public?

 . . . you will be in a much better position to determine when it is likely that you are going to need to deliver the shelving for those stores. If the contact is covering for some other obstacle, you may eventually get a straight answer by trying to focus on the specifics of the matter. That straight answer is likely to sound like this: "Here's the thing, our budgets are frozen until the middle of April."

Question 227: I really didn't anticipate that you'd say that. Why is that an important issue for you?

Use this in situations where you get a vague or incomprehensible late-stage negative response from the prospect. (For example, "I'm concerned about quality.") The goal with this question is simply to get the person to offer more information, hopefully in the form of a story that will illustrate the concern in detail.

Question 228: I realized I built the wrong plan for you. Can I meet with you on Tuesday at 2:00 and show you the new plan we've come up with?

Use this in situations where the prospect promises to give you a final decision at a certain point in time, then mysteriously evaporates into the ozone layer.

Let's be honest—sometimes people try to deliver their bad news by not delivering it at all. If your prospect sends you all kinds of "let's work together" signals for three meetings, then gets word from the president of the company that she wants to go in a totally different direction, the person may not be excited about filling you in on exactly what's happened.

Instead of calling up and asking, "So—did you decide yet?" (a call prospects hate to get), use this question. By accepting "responsibility" for the "wrong plan," you'll get either a new Next Step or a better explanation of what's going on.

If you're having trouble establishing voice-to-voice contact with your prospect, you should consider leaving a brief voice mail message that includes this question. Be sure to supply your return call number.

A good variation is:

Question 229: I've been working on a plan with ABC Company, and I thought their plan might work better for you. Can we get together to discuss it on Tuesday at 2:00?

Suppose you have had three good meetings with the prospect, who assured you that it was "only a formality" that the boss would approve your deal. Somehow, though, three weeks have gone by, and you have gotten no word. Make this call (or leave this message)—and say, "Hey, there must have been something wrong. I was talking to a different company and they had something new that I want to try. I would like to go over a revision on the old plan with you and your boss."

With Questions 228 and 229, you may well find that the prospect will defend the existing plan, but will tell you where the problem actually is in the sale. Your prospect might say, "You know what, the boss never got back to me."

At that point you should ask:

Question 230: Well, can you and I meet with your boss next Tuesday at 2:00?

If that doesn't fly, you should ask:

Question 231: Why don't we set up a conference call so all three of us can go over the plan together—and see whether what I found out from ABC Company is relevant?

Obviously, a face-to-face meeting is preferable, but if this is the only option, take it.

Question 232: We haven't heard from you in a while. Did we do something wrong?

A variation on Question 221, designed for use with an existing customer. Use this question to reinvigorate a relationship with a client you have not heard from in a while. It is considerably cheaper, of course, to hold on to a current client than it is to find a brand-new one. With that in mind, you should probably ask some variation on this question to any customer whose sudden absence is troubling to you. It is a great way to find what is going on in the other person's world, and the same dynamic applies. Nine times out of ten, your customer will correct you by saying, "No, you didn't do anything wrong, it's just that we have been dealing with this crisis here and we've been distracted." (Or some such reaction that gives you some insight into what is going on in the other person's world.)

Regardless, you will get a clearer picture of the forces and pressures that your prospect is facing, and you'll have a great opportunity to request a meeting.

It is possible, of course, that you *did* do something wrong, but just don't know what it is. In that case, asking this question has a very good likelihood of pointing you toward exactly what happened, and will also leave you well positioned to schedule a face-to-face meeting so you can evaluate exactly what took place and how your organization can work to help keep it from happening again. (Note: In such a situation I do strongly recommend trying to find a way to schedule a *face-to-face* meeting with the customer who got less than your best.)

Question 233: My boss would like to pay for you to come out here, meet him, and tour our facility. Can we do that?

Save this for the potentially huge account (or huge current customer) you know you are about to lose to a competitor. (Clear it with your boss first, of course.)

This kind of trip to "meet my boss" almost always unearths fresh information, and will sometimes rescue the sale for you. Changing the locale and getting another meeting is of paramount importance in this situation. As a general, but fairly reliable rule, you will get different and better information on a second meeting than you will on the first, and different and better information on the third meeting than you got on the second. You will also get different and better information by changing locales for the second and subsequent meeting, and you can usually rely on getting even higher quality information if the prospect makes the effort of coming to your facilities to make an in-person visit with you or the senior representatives of your company.

Question 234: I was just thinking of you, and I'd like to see what you're up to these days. Can we get together?

A less intense—and perhaps slightly easier to ask—variation on Question 232. This question, like that one, is designed for current customers who haven't been ordering from you lately.

You really don't need a "reason" to call a key customer and ask for a meeting to catch up on what's going on, of course.

Chapter Ten

Questions That Will Help You Formalize the Sales Decision . . . and Negotiate the Best Deal

An entire book could be written on the various questions a salesperson should be prepared to ask before, during, and after the negotiation process. I am going to offer just a few of the most important questions here, but before you look at them, I want you to consider the possibility that the negotiation process really begins *the moment you walk in the door.*

After all, you are not simply negotiating for price, or for a certain delivery time, or for a particular product mix, or service commitment. You are also negotiating for the prospect's investment to meet with you for the very first time, and you are negotiating for his or her willingness to help spread your message throughout the organization. If you think you are not "negotiating" when you ask a prospect to make a commitment of time, energy, and internal political capital, then you have a very different understanding of negotiating than I do.

Still, there are certain points that come up late in the sales cycle that benefit from intelligent questioning, especially when it comes to more complex deals for products and services. We are talking, at this point, about issues that can either go our way or go the prospect's way—issues that will formalize the prospect's decision to use our product or service.

Once we are reasonably certain that we are going to be doing business with a certain contact, we have to put together a negotiating and closing strategy that is right for our company and our future customer. I offer the following questions, not as a final word on the subject of negotiation, but as representative examples of intelligent questioning during the later phases of the sale. That's really all negotiating is for a salesperson, I believe: asking the right to formalize the key elements of the deal, and making it easy for the other person to use what you offer in a way that benefits both sides.

Question 235: Just out of curiosity, how did you get that figure?

Louis B. Mayer once said of Charlie Chaplin, "Chaplin is no business man . . . he just knows that he can't accept a dollar less."

It is quite common to run into negotiators who adopt much the same approach in their final discussions about a given deal. They have no real strong strategic goal; they know only that they cannot afford to take less than X.

This question allows you to step back from the saber-rattling and work together to identify meaningful comparisons.

It should go without saying that *you* should be able to justify your price by citing past deals with other clients in the same industry or a comparable one.

Question 236: Just out of curiosity, how did you handle pricing questions/issues last time?

Use this if the prospect is intent on sticking to an arbitrary pricing figure, and your attempt to identify meaningful benchmarks and standards goes nowhere.

This is one of four critical information-gathering questions you must be prepared to ask at this stage. The others are . . .

Question 237: How did you handle invoicing/terms last time?

And . . .

Question 238: How did you pick the (specific product/service, or element of the product/service) last time?

And . . .

Question 239: What was your timetable for implementation the last time you did this (or: did something like this)?

These four questions are also vitally important to the success of your discussions. At any given moment, your negotiating discussion is likely to center on one of four critical questions from the prospect:

- How much will it cost?
- When do I have to pay?
- What product or service am I offering?
- What is the implementation timetable?

If you don't know what the benchmarks were for the last similar purchasing decision the company made in each of these areas, *you are negotiating at a disadvantage.*

To be sure, the prospect may choose not to share some of this information with you. But you have gotten this far by asking intelligent questions. Why stop now?

When you are pressured on any of these points during the later phases of a sales discussion—price, invoicing, product/service offering or availability; or delivery dates/implementation; it *always* makes sense to disengage and get the relevant facts about the person's past experience in the area in which you are working.

If there is no precise equivalent, disengage a little more, then ask your prospect what he or she thinks is the most likely situation he or she has faced.

The point is to encourage your contact to step back from a "hard-line" position, and also to identify, if possible, the relevant benchmarks you can both use to discuss what the final package would look like.

Question 240: Can we come back to this?

An *extremely* important negotiating question. If you don't ask it at least once, you are not doing your job well.

If you have an impasse on one of those three things, you can always step back and ask to look at one of the other three elements.

If an issue is only producing disagreement and frustration, there is no sin in asking that it be postponed in order to allow you and the prospect to discuss something that you do agree on. Emphasize commonalities, and you will eventually be able to build up enough trust to move forward to the most difficult issues.

It is also true that by postponing the most difficult issues, at least with someone whom you know to be committed to finding a way to work out a deal, you may improve your negotiation position. But this depends, to a large degree, on who really has the most control of the negotiating session. If you have reason to suspect the prospect will in fact walk away if you put off discussing *X* for too long, and you don't want the person to walk away, you're probably going to have to discuss *X* sooner rather than later.

Question 241: Okay—how were you planning on paying for it?

Use this to get a sense of the other side's priorities when your organization's payment terms are under assault. Don't just volunteer to improve the terms; ask, specifically, what kind of terms the other side has in mind.

Question 242: Why those terms?

If the answer to Question 241 is not something you can sell to your boss, explore the reasoning behind the terms suggested by the other side. Is it based on past experience with other vendors—or is it the kind of request one places on one's Christmas list, while hoping for a visit from Santa?

Question 243: Did you have any problems with (*X*) last time?

Use this question to spotlight the value your company delivers in a given area that a competitor probably did not deliver in the past. For instance: If you know the deal the prospect negotiated last time around included a lousy maintenance program, and you know your company delivers a superior maintenance package, you should emphasize (or perhaps subtly re-emphasize) the value you will be delivering.

Question 244: How much do you think those problems ended up costing your organization?

A necessary follow-up to Question 243. If specialized technical help, additional repairs, reduced effectiveness, or lost customers resulted from the problems you identified in Question 243, you should use this query to quantify how much that problem ultimately cost the prospect, in hard-dollar terms. If you have expertise, support, or other resources that will keep your prospect from experiencing that loss again, you should not be shy about emphasizing that dollar figure, and pointing out that it is not part of the cost—direct or indirect—of doing business with you.

Question 245: Is it too low?

A good tension-reducing question you should pose—with a straight face—when the prospect says "We've got a problem on price."

Don't underestimate the role humor can play in establishing a good emotional atmosphere for your negotiating session. This very joke can lighten the mood with a "hard-as-nails" negotiator, and lead you to a win-win outcome.

Question 246: What did you think the number was going to be?

This is a good question to ask if the prospect reacts negatively when you are placed in the position of naming your price first. It is a marked improvement over looking for opportunities to offer discounts.

I came in contact once with a salesperson who sold over the phone. He was so used to getting price resistance from his prospects that he actually offered to discount when one of his prospects agreed to buy! It was simply a knee-jerk reaction, an instinctive response. Do not let that happen to you. Before you agree to, or even consider, discounting, ask the other person what figure he or she was looking for. Do not move on until you get some kind of meaningful response.

Question 247: Let's assume that I come up with a great program/product for you, and it costs ($X). Would you buy it?

It should go without saying that you will not want to volunteer prices along the lines suggested here until you are well into the discussions with your prospect.

With that warning out of the way, I do want to emphasize that your goal in the negotiation phase should be finding *something* that will work for this organization, at this time, through this series of discussions. This question can be an effective tool for identifying what that something is.

Reconfiguring Your Offer

I am a big believer in reshuffling and reconfiguring my offering during the negotiation phase. I will never simply discount my price, but I will, as suggested in the earlier question, throw out a different price to determine whether or not it will work for the prospect. Once I determine that it will, I will go back to the drawing board and redraw and rearrange my offering, taking elements out and putting new elements in, so that I can find a new and different mix that will work for this prospect in this situation.

This is an important exercise, and one that I think every salesperson with negotiating responsibilities should practice. How many different ways can you bundle your product or service? How many different ways can you put together the various elements, and still deliver superior value, but for a different price? It is a guiding principle in the world of effective negotiation that you never give up something for nothing. So, if a prospect demands a significant price concession, the best advice is not simply to say, "Yes," but to identify the price plan that will work for him or her, and come back with a new offering that matches that price.

Knowing When to Walk Away

As you walk into the negotiating session, it is your responsibility to know precisely when, and under what circumstances, you will walk away from the negotiations. That is not the prospect's job—it is yours. If the other side suggests, and insists on, a price, plan, or package that is simply beyond the criteria you are willing to accept, you really should politely conclude the negotiations and walk out.

The unstated, but perhaps obvious, principle underlying this advice is that the more business you have waiting for you, the more favorable the offer you can demand during negotiating sessions. I like to remind salespeople during our training sessions that prospecting for new leads is not simply a way of initiating new business relationships; it is also a silent bit of leverage that you can use to justify a decision to move on to a new deal. If you have no prospects, your negotiating position will be poor.

Your Questioning Strategy

Identify, ahead of time, the point at which you are willing to walk away. Be prepared to walk away if you do not get that deal.

Question 248: Can we set up a pilot/introductory/mini program?

If discussions are in danger of getting seriously bogged down, consider the possibility of offering a miniature version of your program as part of a pilot offering. This may be easier for the prospect to agree to, and there is very little downside on your part, as long as you are there to help implement it and also to help interpret the results of the program. The bottom line: Use this to get the first deal, even if small, across the finish line. Then be sure to stay involved throughout the course of the pilot program!

Question 249: If I do *X*, do we have a deal?

Definitely a late-stage question. Do not be afraid to ask for clarification on exactly what stands between you and the deal. There is no crime in being specific, or in asking someone else to do so.

Once you've posed the question, stop talking and see what response comes back.

Question 250: It makes sense to me—what do you think?

This is the question that we have been working our way up to throughout the entire sales process, and indeed throughout the course of this book. It is, ultimately, the only question that matters.

I have included it here as the question you can use to "clinch the deal," and it is certainly the most effective strategy I have ever come across for doing that. It is also, however, the underlying question behind just about everything else you have read here.

Sales is a matter of throwing the ball. If I toss a ball to you, you have to react somehow. You can let the ball drop to the floor; you can catch it and throw it back to me; you can catch it and take it away. But you do have to do something. This question, for all its simplicity, *is* that act of throwing the sales "ball," condensed to a few simple words. It is the question you should ask when you want to execute the plan you believe, in your heart, to be in the best interests of both parties.

On its own, however, it is useless. If you simply deliver a memorized "spiel" for half an hour, and turn to the person and say, "It makes sense to me. What do you think?" you will not be selling at the optimum level. You will, of course, close some sales—the sales to the people who are already in the marketplace, and who are already predisposed to buying, and who have more or less made up their mind to buy from someone. Those sales will come your way no matter what. But in order to get to the highest level of sales, you must be willing to ask some variation of this question *throughout* the process, not merely at the end.

Does it make sense for the person to meet with you in the first place? Does it make sense for him or her to allow you to interview key people within the organization? Does it make sense for him or her to share personal insights and experiences—the "stories" that have made this person a unique asset to his or her organization? Does it make sense for this person to share sensitive reports and data with you? Does it make sense for him or her to go out on a limb and introduce you to the president of the company? Does it make sense to him or her to meet with you a second or third or fourth time? Does it make sense to him or her to allow you to develop the presentations that will be delivered before the all-important committee meeting?

All these questions and their hundreds of potential variations are the necessary precursors to this question.

Don't just ask the final question . . . ask all the questions that lead up to it and make it possible. That way, if the recommendation you are making really does make sense, you will be in a great position, not only to close a sale, but to build a future.

List of Questions

Chapter Three: *Opening* **Questions to Figure Out What the Person and the Company Do**

31. I checked our records, and I noticed that you are not working with us. Why not?
32. I am just curious. Have you ever worked with a company like ours before?
33. What made you want to consider (widgets)?
34. Have you ever reached out to a company like ours before? If so, who was it? Why them?
35. Mr. Jones, my guess is that you are an XYZ customer. What made you choose them?
36. How did you choose ABC?
37. What is the main thing that you are trying to accomplish this month/quarter/year?
38. What is the main thing that your CEO/president/boss is trying to accomplish this month/quarter/year?
39. What kind of person is your CEO?
40. What made you decide to call us?
41. What were you going to do about your (widget) problem if I had not called you?
42. Just out of curiosity, whom do you consider to be your important competition?
43. How do you think you stack up against the competition?
44. How do you distinguish yourself in an industry like this?
45. How do you maintain a competitive edge in an industry as tough as this one?

46. How do you set yourself apart from your competition?
47. What are you doing right now to . . . ?
48. What are you doing right now to control your telecom costs and to keep people connected?
49. What are you doing right now to train your salespeople?
50. What are you doing right now to retain your key people?
51. What are you doing right now for employee orientation?
52. What are you doing right now to deal with the competitive pressures that your salespeople face in this industry?
53. What are you doing right now to track and manage your overseas shipments?
54. Just so I know where we are headed, what is the main thing you want your vendor to accomplish here?
55. What were your goals for today's meeting?
56. How do you plan to . . . ?
57. How do you plan to reach out to (prospective franchisees)?
58. What is your plan for (cutting down on your heating bill costs this winter—have you thought about that at all)?
59. What are you doing right now to keep (your heating costs down)?
60. What is your plan for (providing coffee service for your employees)?
61. What are you planning to do to (retain your key people)?

62. If I worked here, how would I get started and what would my first week look like?

63. My guess is, your people face challenge X. What do you think?

64. Why do you think that's happening?

65. Sometimes people have a problem with (X). What's your take on that?

66. Other people in your industry have told me (X). Is that your experience?

Chapter Four: *Follow-Through* Questions to Figure Out What the Person and the Company Do

67. "So—are you currently . . . ?" (the Framed Question)

68. I've spoken to your counterparts in other industries and they've got a preference for blue widgets. Have you found that to be the case?

69. A lot of the people I've spoken to in the shipping industry have told me that they feel that prospects for expanding in the European market are very limited. What's your take on that?

70. You don't mind if I take notes, do you?

71. Who did you work with last time?

72. Why them?

73. Did you ever think about working with us?

74. How did you decide to handle challenge X the last time it came up with your vendor?

75. Just to get a ballpark figure, what kind of budget are you working with?

76. Gee, I'm surprised to hear you say that. Usually people are very happy to tell me what kind of budget to work with, at least in general numbers so we can talk about a price range. Why wouldn't we want to talk about that?

77. What is your timeline?

78. If you and I were to decide to work together, what would the calendar for that look like?

79. What is your average sales cycle?

80. Do you personally do a lot of (long-distance calling)? (Assuming that you are selling telecommunications.)

81. What kinds of concerns do you personally have about (the team's performance)?

82. What kind of concerns do you have about hitting your sales quota this year?

83. What kind of concerns do you have about managing your communications with your sales force during the time that the merger is underway?

84. What kind of concerns do you have about reaching out to the Eastern European market?

85. What are the biggest challenges you personally are facing with this project?

86. Why is that the biggest challenge?

87. A lot of your counterparts at organizations in this industry have told me that their biggest personnel challenge when it comes to salespeople is developing the right incentive program. Is that your experience as well?

88. Who is your ideal customer?

89. What kinds of new customers are you trying to attract?

90. How would you describe your ideal customer?

91. Who is your most important prospect right now?

92. What is your most important target market?

93. What are you trying to do to reach that market?

94. Who are your most important suppliers/vendors?

95. How long have you been with the company?

96. How do you like the job?

97. What is it like to work here?

98. How many people work in this department/division/branch?

99. How many of these people report to you?

100. How many of these people work with you?

101. How many other locations do you have?

102. Can I tell you a little bit about why I chose to work with this company?

103. Can I tell you a little bit about why XYZ Company decided to work with us?

104. Who would you say is your most important competitor?

105. Where do you think the economy is going?

106. Where do you think this industry is going?

107. Does your company have any plans to expand?

108. How is your company dealing with the challenges in this industry?

109. How do you think (problem X/challenge X) happened?

110. How did you end up with the system you're using now?

111. How did this (system) get (installed/tested/analyzed)?

112. How do you see (X) problem?

113. Have you ever worked with an outsider on a project like this before?

114. How long have you been trying to . . . ?

115. Just out of curiosity, what makes this a top priority for you personally?

116. What would you think is the most important project/initiative you are working on right now?

117. How does this initiative affect your salespeople and your marketing efforts?

118. How does this initiative affect your logistics and operations team?

119. How does this initiative affect your recruiting or retention efforts?

120. How does your company sell its products or services?

121. How important are repeat sales to your company?

122. What are you doing to hold on to your best customers?
123. How are you going to use this?
124. What are you doing right now to improve your profile in the marketplace?
125. Can I tell you what some of your counterparts in the organizations that we have been working with are concerned about in this area?
126. Can I tell you how some of my clients in the (X) industry dealt with this problem?
127. Can I share with you how we handled this when we faced a similar situation with (ABC Company)? Or Can I give you the highlights of a case study we did that was very similar to this?
128. Can I tell you about something that happened to me that may be helpful?
129. Can I tell you what my boss did about this when he faced the same situation?
130. Can I tell you why I ask that question?
131. What is on the horizon?

Chapter Five: Questions to Figure Out What Someone Who Contacts *You* Does

132. Just out of curiosity, what made you decide to call us?
133. Can I ask how you heard about us?
134. Had you ever thought about working with us before?

135. I'm just curious, what made you decide to get in touch with us about . . . ?
136. I'm just curious, what made you decide to take action in this area?
137. I'm just curious, what made you decide to get a quote for (replacing the windows in your home)?
138. By the way, have you heard about our . . . ?
139. What made you decide to stop by today?
140. Hi there, I'm Mike. Are you looking for something for your (husband)?
141. Oh, okay—just out of curiosity, has your (son) got (anything to wear for formal dances)?
142. Do you see anything you can't absolutely live without?
143. I didn't think so. (Little pause.) Can I show you something?
144. When are you going back?
145. What does the company do? Or Who are its customers?
146. Who are you talking to?
147. Why that person?
148. How long has your contact been there?
149. What, specifically, is this company doing now in an area where we can add value?
150. Why aren't they using us already?
151. When was your first meeting?
152. Did you call them or did they call you?
153. How much is the deal worth?

154. In your view, what is the very next thing that has to happen for you to eventually close this sale?
155. When and how will you make that happen?
156. Who else are they looking at?
157. Why them?
158. What does your contact think is going to happen next?
159. When is that going to happen?
160. Do they want this deal to happen as much as you do?

Chapter Six: Questions That Move You Toward a Next Step

161. Can we meet next Tuesday at 2:00—so I can show you an outline of how we might be able to work together?
162. Okay, Mr. Prospect, I think we are thinking along the same lines—at least I hope we are. Here is what I want to do next. I would like to go back to my office and share what you have told me about your recruitment goals with some of the senior people at my company, and then what I want to do is brainstorm with them and give them the opportunity to share their insights on how we might be able to put together a plan for you. I don't think we are ready to look at a proposal yet, but what I do think we are in the position to do is show you an outline. I would like to come back here next Tuesday at 10:00 just to show you some of our initial thinking on what might go into the proposal, and then I would like to meet with some of the other people on your team who might be able to help us develop the program more fully. Does that make sense?
163. Why wouldn't you want to meet next week?
164. Wow—I am kind of surprised to hear you say that. Usually by this point in the meeting, people are very eager to meet with us again. Just out of curiosity, why wouldn't you want get together again to look at our outline?
165. Can I meet with your team and report back to you on (May 31)?
166. Why don't we get my boss to meet your boss?
167. Why don't I set up a conference call so you can talk to one of our customers?
168. Why don't you come to one of our company events?
169. Why don't you come take a look at our facility?
170. Can I get a tour of your facility?
171. Why don't I come back and show you . . . ?
172. Why don't I do an online presentation for your key people?
173. Why don't we set a time now to debrief about the online presentation?

174. Why don't you and I meet with my boss?
175. Why don't you and I meet with our technical expert? Or Why don't we get your technical people together with my technical people?
176. How do you (upload your two-dimensional widget projections)?
177. What do you think we should do next?
178. Whom do you want me to talk to next?
179. Can I keep you in the loop?
180. Is there someone else in your industry whom you think I should be talking to?

Chapter Seven: "Next Step" Questions for Managers Only

181. Do you have enough first appointments?
182. How many of your meetings this week are taking place within the time frame of your average selling cycle?
183. How many new prospects do you have for this week as compared to last week?
184. Is your activity in balance?
185. In scheduling your next week's activity, what is the best territory management approach?
186. Who can I call for you?
187. What is your goal for the next meeting with this person?
188. How will you open the next meeting?
189. What Next Step strategy will you use to get back?

Chapter Eight: Questions That Help You Identify and Deliver the Right Presentation

190. Before we get started, can I share with you what I got from our last meeting?
191. Before we begin, can I share what I discussed with my boss/team/manager about our last meeting?
192. Has anything changed since our last meeting?
193. Did you have a chance to talk to anyone else in the organization about what we discussed last time?
194. Just to get some feedback on this outline, why don't you and I set up a meeting/conference call with . . . ?
195. Are we thinking along the same lines in terms of price?
196. Is this product/service what you are looking for?
197. Have I got the timing about right?
198. I'm sensing that there is a problem somewhere— where did I go off track?
199. I feel as if I'm missing something—what do you think I'm missing here?
200. That's how I would put what we're trying to do—but how would you put it?
201. Just between you and me, what do you really think is going to happen here?
202. Can I make a presentation directly to the committee (team/work group)?

203. I'm surprised to hear you say that. Why wouldn't you want me to talk before the committee (team/work group)?

204. What can you tell me about how the committee works?

205. How will the final decision be made after the committee meets?

206. Who would we be presenting to?

207. How was the committee formed?

208. When did the committee first meet?

209. How should we reach out to the people on the committee?

210. Can you and I set up a time to debrief right now?

211. What do you think (person X) will think about what we've put together?

212. How many good copies should I put together/bring?

213. Just between you and me, what do you think the result of the meeting is going to be?

214. Can I build the presentation for you?

215. Can I put together a first draft of the presentation for you?

Chapter Nine: Questions That Deal with Setbacks or Obstacles in the Sales Process

216. Just out of curiosity . . . what makes you think that's the right figure/date/deal?

217. What makes you say that?

218. What were you expecting?

219. Can I tell you how we handled this issue when I worked with Company X?

220. Did I do something wrong here?

221. Mr. Prospect, I have to be honest with you. Something is wrong here. Usually, when I have gotten this far through the process of meeting with someone, people are very excited about what I have recommended, and they do, in fact, decide to work with us. Actually, I pride myself on not making a recommendation until I am really sure that the other person is more excited about it than I am. I know for a fact that we have got the best program for you, and that it will deliver the results that you and I spoke about. So, I have to assume that I have done something wrong in outlining this plan for you. So help me out. Did I do something wrong? If I did—what was it?

222. You know, usually, by this point in my meeting with somebody, I get a lot more interaction and a lot more excitement about what I am discussing. And I get the feeling I really have not done that with you today. Did I do something wrong?

223. Did (name) do something wrong?

224. I get the feeling you are not really happy with what I've proposed here. Am I right?

225. Let me ask you something— by what point in time are you trying to achieve (X)?

226. When do you want your new stores to be open to the public?

227. I really didn't anticipate that you'd say that. Why is that an important issue for you?

228. I realized I built the wrong plan for you. Can I meet with you on Tuesday at 2:00 and show you the new plan we've come up with?

229. I've been working on a plan with ABC Company, and I thought their plan might work better for you. Can we get together to discuss it on Tuesday at 2:00?

230. Well, can you and I meet with your boss next Tuesday at 2:00?

231. Why don't we set up a conference call so all three of us can go over the plan together—and see whether what I found out from ABC Company is relevant?

232. We haven't heard from you in a while. Did we do something wrong?

233. My boss would like to pay for you to come out here, meet him, and tour our facility. Can we do that?

234. I was just thinking of you, and I'd like to see what you're up to these days. Can we get together?

Chapter Ten: Questions That Help You Formalize the Sales Decision . . . and Negotiate the Best Deal

235. Just out of curiosity, how did you get that figure?

236. Just out of curiosity, how did you handle pricing questions/issues last time?

237. How did you handle invoicing/terms last time?

238. How did you pick the (specific product/service, or element of the product/service) last time?

239. What was your timetable for implementation the last time you did this (or: did something like this)?

240. Can we come back to this?

241. Okay—how were you planning on paying for it?

242. Why those terms?

243. Did you have any problems with (X) last time?

244. How much do you think those problems ended up costing your organization?

245. Is it too low?

246. What did you think the number was going to be?

247. Let's assume that I come up with a great program/product/offering for you, and it costs ($X). Would you buy it?

248. Can we set up a pilot/introductory/mini program?

249. If I do X, do we have a deal?

250. It makes sense to me— what do you think?

Index